Cristina Pozzi | Young Global Leaders 2019-2024 of the World Economic Forum

DESTINATION 2050

A Practical Guide to the Future

Cover: Studio Wise, Milano
Typesetting: Laura Panigara, Cesano Boscone (MI)

Copyright © 2020 Bocconi University Press
EGEA S.p.A.

EGEA S.p.A.
Via Salasco, 5 - 20136 Milano
Tel. 02/5836.5751 – Fax 02/5836.5753
egea.edizioni@unibocconi.it – www.egeaeditore.it

All rights reserved, including but not limited to translation, total or partial adaptation, reproduction, and communication to the public by any means on any media (including microfilms, films, photocopies, electronic or digital media), as well as electronic information storage and retrieval systems. For more information or permission to use material from this text, see the website www.egeaeditore.it

Given the characteristics of Internet, the publisher is not responsible for any changes of address and contents of the websites mentioned.

First edition: January 2020

ISBN Domestic Edition   978-88-99902-70-4
ISBN International Edition   978-88-85486-97-3
ISBN Epub and Mobipocket International Edition 978-88-85486-98-2

*This book is for my three beautiful nieces
and all the young people in the world:
the future is yours, and it's our responsibility
to give you the best possible 2050.
Let's travel there together.*

Table of Contents

Preliminary Remarks. Preparing for the Future	1
Singularity and transhumanism	2
Epochal passages	3
Leaving for the trip	6
The structure of the book	8
Acknowledgements	8
Ten things not to be missed	10
1 Snapshot of 2050	13
The inhabitants	13
Inhabited places	22
Culture	25
The alphabet of the new generations	27
Anthropocene	29
The political landscape	32
Currency	46
Society, work and education	54
Love, reproduction and relationships	68
2 Practical Information	81
The climate	81
Animals and nature	86
Religious rites	89
No language barriers	90
Food	91
Sport and leisure time	105
Children	124

	Health	124
	Transportation	133
3	**Preparing for the Trip**	145
	Passports and documents	145
	Emergencies	145
	(Lost and) found	146
	Communication	146
	Compatibility of technological devices	148
	Hospitality	148
4	**The Future**	151
	The future is always with us	151
	Creating the future by telling stories	154
	Technology and inventions	155
	Responsibility	156

Glossary of the Future 157

Bibliography 165

Preliminary Remarks

Preparing for the Future

The date is July 27, 2017. The smell of sulphur is almost unbearable, it's hellishly hot and my feet seem to be on fire. I'm standing on a volcanic hill, gazing across an infinite landscape, shaped by the lava flows that have followed one another over the millennia and that time has transformed into more or less rounded hills. A few hours ago, before climbing this hill, I stopped in awe at the wonder of a lake made turquoise by the sulphur present in its boiling waters. I'm in Iceland. I've dreamt of this journey to a land where nature expresses itself in all its indomitable power since I was a child.

For years I have studied the natural wonders that I could admire, breathe and touch with my own hands. For years I've been imagining what it would be like to be here. I was able to feed my imagination thanks to the pictures, videos, documentaries and stories of those who made the trip before me, and I planned my own journey by reading tourist guides in search of valuable advice.

Was the experience exactly as I expected?

I'd say not. I can't cope with the amount of natural sunshine that floods this mixed land. Improvised detours are among the most surprising things. I was wrong about something, that's for sure. My feet hurt – I should have brought lighter shoes to combat the heat as well as heavier ones for the glaciers – and I realize my suitcase is full of useless items. But each choice was guided by a mental model, well trained over the years, which allowed me to know in advance the rules of the world I was going to explore, and to move with relative confidence, even in the face of unforeseen events.

I stop for a moment to imagine the same journey made without any preparation. What if I woke up without even knowing that Iceland exists and found myself here, at the top of the hill, as a result of magic, after falling asleep quietly at my house last night? How long would it take me to understand where I am and to assess opportunities and dangers? On what will I base the choices I have to make? What if I suddenly found myself in some kind of trouble?

Singularity and transhumanism

To be in 2050 without adequate preparation would most probably have just this effect, multiplied a thousand times, since it would be an almost incomprehensible reality for us. But why should we expect such radical changes in little more than thirty years? The concept of *technological singularity* provides a start to finding an answer.

It was in 1993 that the idea was first proposed that sooner or later scientific advances would mean we would find ourselves in a reality beyond human understanding. That very year, Vernor Vinge, an award-winning science fiction writer who had formerly been a mathematics professor at San Diego State University, published a scientific article entitled "The Coming Technological Singularity: How to Survive in the Post-Human Era".[1]

Singularity in physics refers to a disruptive event that can change everything in an instant. According to this definition, for example, the Big Bang is a moment of singularity. Adding the concept of technology, with particular regard to artificial intelligence, and abstracting from physics, we find ourselves talking about a *radical change* that intimately affects our humanity: a singularity in the cognitive abilities of human beings.

Vinge's reasoning is highly logical: by 2030 we will be able to create intelligences superior to ourselves. Afterwards, these intelligences will in turn be able to do the same, leading to an unstoppable process that will make reality as incomprehensible to human beings today as our civilization is to a goldfish.[2]

The concept has been taken up by the futurist Ray Kurzweil who, in addition to having written widely on the subject of technological acceptance and the consequent approach of the moment of singularity, has even created, together with the innovator Peter Diamandis, a training centre called Singularity University.[3] Kurzweil, adding about fifteen years to Vinge's prediction, initially assumed that the moment of singularity would come in 2045, but later indicated a much nearer date: 2029.

So if Vinge and Kurzweil are right, in 2050 we would be in a very different place from today, and without proper guidance we would feel overwhelmed.

The discussion on singularity is split into two main viewpoints: those who argue that it will inevitably be something unique in the history of mankind, and those who believe that the expected changes will not be very different from those that have occurred in the past, with the advent, for example, of the printing press.

According to the former, the only way not to be overwhelmed by the tsunami of change would be to take our evolution into our own hands and intentionally direct it towards *technological, genetic and chemical enhancements* so as to ensure we are superior to the intelligent machines we have created. What does this mean? Enhancing humans, for the supporters of this thesis, means resorting to DNA manipulation, chemistry and neurotechnologies to increase our cognitive abilities through fusing ourselves with technology. After all, don't a little makeup, a pair of glasses, a pen, a calculator or a computer serve the same purpose?

This type of philosophy is called *transhumanism* and according to most of its followers it seems that in the future there will be no room for those who fall behind. In response to the perplexity of those who highlight the dividing power of this vision, James Hughes, in his book *Citizen Cyborg*,[4] explains how the democratic societies of the future will be able to create a world without inequalities even after the advent of new branches of the human species, such as those potentially arising from this approach, which involves intentionally directing our evolution. In 2050, the subject will certainly be very topical, as we shall see in the pages of this book.

Singularity and transhumanism are therefore deeply linked and from the theoretical point of view they reinforce each other: the first provides the basis for showing the necessity of the second.

Epochal passages

As anticipated, not everyone agrees with this vision. We will certainly see enormous changes due to the development of technologies and innovations such as artificial intelligence, robotics, 3D printing, blockchain technologies, quantum computing, nanotechnology, biotechnology, advances in genetics and space exploration. It is certain that these changes will require humanity to review the institutions and pillars of society. It is also true, however, that our past is studded with great epochal passages in which our society has been called into question and has undergone radical changes.

For those in favour of the concept of singularity, therefore, the change we are facing is only possible at certain times, such as the advent of our species on the planet, for the others we are faced with something similar to the invention of the printing press and we are in the middle of a passage from one era to another. We could say we're on a *trans-epochal Journey*. In this case understanding at least some of the rules of the game could be helpful.

The passages from one epoch to another are moments in the history of mankind in which we find ourselves between two distinct periods (usually realized a posteriori) in a very clear way, as a result of their unique cultural and social characteristics. These moments are characterized by changes that instead of being linear and continuous – and therefore predictable – are discontinuous and difficult to predict.

At this point, the typical objection offered by those who support singularity and transhumanism is that the difference today is caused by speed, so-called *technological acceleration*. The fact that the pace of change and changes due to the impacts of technologies are much faster than a few centuries ago, thanks to the Internet revolution and its spread, is beyond dispute. However, this is also an incremental process such as we have seen in the past, with the advent of particularly revolutionary technologies such as printing. Reading some of the works of the time we find ourselves perceiving the same sensations. Here, for example, is what Tommaso Campanella wrote at the turn of the sixteenth century: "There has been more *history* in a hundred years that the world did not have in four thousand; and more books were made in these hundred than in five thousand; and the stupendous inventions of the magnet and prints and arquebuses, great signs of the union of the world."[5] In the same period Pierre Borel expressed himself as follows: "We would certainly have been incredulous if they had assured us that, through printing, it would have been possible 'to write an infinity of books in a short time and at a speed infinitely faster than speech ... thus acquiring a sort of immortality.'"[6] Do these statements not remind you of certain phrases made viral by social networks? "Every day we create 2.5 quintiles of data bytes. To put it into context: 90% of the data in the world today has only been created in the last two years. And

PRELIMINARY REMARKS

with new devices, sensors and emerging technologies, the rate of data growth is likely to accelerate even faster."[7]

Reports and analyses like the one by IBM from which this quote is taken are very fashionable today and highlight exactly what Campanella and Borel already pointed out: technology and human inventions speed up processes and thus increase the speed of our interactions and activities. Today we are faced with revolutions concerning data and our ability to analyse and use it as a decision-making tool, concerning increasingly large and connected social networks thanks to the Internet and concerning scientific advances that allow us to begin to understand life and our biological body as never before. The convergence of these revolutions will determine our future. But what will be the extent of that change?

Let's go back to those who believe that we are in the middle of what we have called a trans-epochal journey. If we were at a moment of transition similar to those experienced in history, we could find useful indications to cope with this in the study of the past, present and future, and, consequently, of the change. At times like the present, however, according to the American Futurist Peter C. Bishop, we find it harder to understand the changes and to predict the future, since the changes are discontinuous,[8] as depicted in Figure 1. In this type of context, the tools of analysis

Figure 1 Epochs and changes

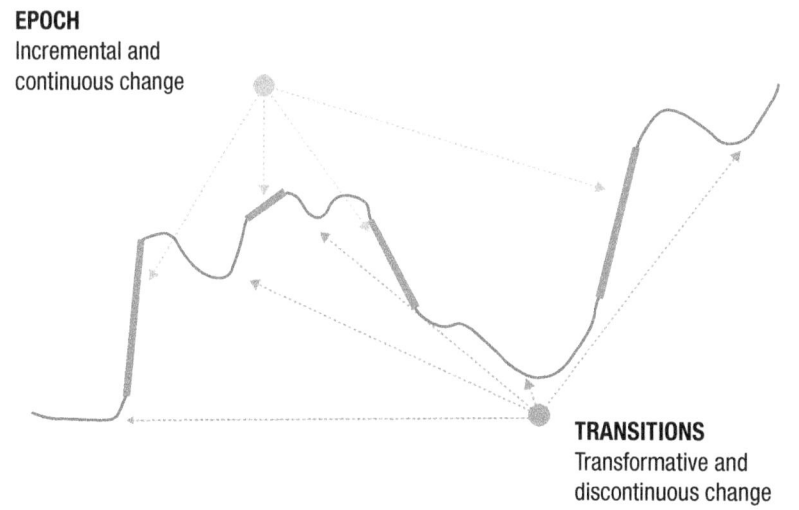

EPOCH
Incremental and
continuous change

TRANSITIONS
Transformative and
discontinuous change

and strategic forecasting that we use to think about linear changes are not valid; however, using the right tools we could also face these transformations with some confidence.

Leaving for the trip

But do we really have to select one theory or the other to understand and guide the future? Can't we usefully find common ground, no matter what our vision?

In my opinion, whether we are close to singularity, or a trans-epochal journey, it would be irresponsible to face the future that awaits us without trying to prepare ourselves using the right tools. So if, like me, you want to know at least something about what awaits you before you embark on your journey into the future, you have the right book in your hand.

Too often we let ourselves be carried away by time, without trying to understand what the reality that we are going to experience in the immediate future will be like. We are blind to the wonders and potential dangers on the horizon for one simple reason: we don't know where to look. Then, suddenly, we find ourselves projected into a new prehearsal, we realize how many things have changed and we find ourselves struggling, unnecessarily, to chase the rhythms of a society for which we are not prepared.

The future is the wildest destination we can ever visit. It is a complex place and time, which requires study and the exercise of the imagination before leaving. The tools are few and uncertain: there are more things that we do not know – that we know we do not know and that we do not know we do not know – than that we really know. And even when we start from the few certainties that we have, we make mistakes, inevitably, because it is impossible to predict the future during an trans-epochal passage of this magnitude.

So, how do you do it?

The first thing is to study, to understand the possible futures that loom before us. Then we have to try to explore them, imagine them, question them. Only then will we have a chance to understand which we really want to visit in person and how to prepare for the trip. Sure, it's exhausting. Creativity, resourcefulness, flexibility and the ability to work in a team are needed to enrich our visions with those of others (who will after all be our travelling companions). You need courage, resilience and a critical spirit. In this way, with imagination, creativity and a critical spirit, we can build speculative scenarios and plausible simulations.

It is with these tools that the book you have in your hands was composed and these are also the things that we will have to put into practice to face the journey towards 2050.

Let us not delude ourselves that it is possible to continue not to think about it: the journey into the future is not a choice. It concerns us all and, in this historical phase of radical change, it is folly to travel unpredictably. The future, with its extraordinary destinations, its unexpected experiences, its extreme complexity, its opportunities and threats, requires profound reflection from everyone before departure, whether they are regular travellers to the future or about to embark on their first journey.

So let's leave together for 2050: a destination far enough away to have experienced great changes in the life of its inhabitants, but also close enough to affect most of us, either personally or through our children or grandchildren.

If you have decided to embark on your journey into the future responsibly, you will find many useful tips on how to leave equipped for a wonderful destination on the following pages. With its multifaceted reality, technological developments and wide range of scenarios to visit, 2050 is a destination that will amaze the most daring travellers, from those who love new things and urban landscapes, to those who are looking for a holiday full of surprises and boundless spaces.

The journey won't be easy. To get used to it, you'll need specific information and tools, a spirit of adventure and a good dose of adaptability. I trust that the contents of this book may suggest an effective strategy to best plan your itinerary, helping you to decide in which direction to go, what future to leave for, what to visit and what to take with you. What do you eat in 2050? How do you dress? Where do young people go to have fun? Where do people live? Which are the biggest cities, which are the experiences not to be missed? How to prepare for the climate? Customs, languages, nutrition, institutions: everything in 2050 will be quite different from the world we are used to. Everything raises questions, fuels hope and increases the weight of our responsibility.

Let us then prepare ourselves to embark on our journey to discover the possible realities of the future. To choose the reality that each one of us would like to see realized, starting from today.

Have a nice trip!

The structure of the book

Welcome to 2050 is the result of the explorations I do every day with the Impactscool team.[9] The wealth of stimuli and ideas that arise daily in this context are reflected in the many curiosities and insights that enrich the text.

Each reader can move among the pages as he or she wishes, letting himself or herself be guided by his or her own interests and needs.

 = Insights

 = Curiosity

 = A jump back to the present

 The "2050 Today" boxes will host a selection of the most curious news that has appeared in the main magazine of the future.

At the end of the book, for those who do not know the language of tomorrow well, a small "Glossary of the future" provides a guide to the essential words in 2050.

Acknowledgements

Travelling into the future is serious: it can be dangerous and exciting.

As with all travel, what makes the difference is the company, and I could never have written this book without my fellow travellers, who made every stage of the journey unforgettable.

And thanks to those who, like my family, have always supported me in my most bizarre missions, hiding their concerns behind a "I recommend prudence" (and in the future it takes a lot).

And thanks to all those who have decided to interact with Impactscool, telling us their vision of the future: this book could not exist without them.

The biggest thanks, however, go to Andrea Dusi: I met you at the start of my journey and you have contributed more than anyone to make it stimulating, fun, challenging. You pushed the boundaries of my curiosity and, above all, you always expressed to me your true opinion, even when you knew I wouldn't like it.

Notes

[1] V. Vinge, "The coming technological singularity: How to survive in the post-human era", conference paper, Department of Mathematical Sciences San Diego State University, 1993 (for the curious, the text can be found on the net).
[2] In an interview published in the transhumanist magazine *H+*, Vinge described the singularity as follows: "I think the term Singularity is appropriate, because unlike other technological changes, it seems to me pretty evident that this change would be unintelligible to us afterwards in the same way that our present civilization is unintelligible to a goldfish" (D. Wolens, "Singularity 101 with Vernor Vinge", *H+ Magazine*, 22 April 2009).
[3] In particular, we can cite R. Kurzweil, *The Singularity is Near: When Humans Transcend Biology*, New York, Viking, 2005.
[4] J. Hughes, *Citizen Cyborg: Why Democratic Societies Must Respond to the Redesigned Human of the Future*, Cambridge (MA), Westview Press, 2004.
[5] T. Campanella, *La città del sole* (1602), edited by N. Bobbio, Turin, Einaudi, 1941, 109.
[6] P. Borel, *Discours nouveau prouvant la pluralité des mondes* (1657), ed. A. Del Prete, Lecce, Conte Editore, 1998.
[7] IBM Marketing Cloud, "10 Key Marketing Trends for 2017 and Ideas for Exceeding Customer Expectations", comsenseconsulting.com, 2017.
[8] P. Bishop, "Framework forecasting. Managing uncertainty and influencing the future", paper presented at Second Prague Workshop on Futures Studies Methodology, October 2005.
[9] Impactscool (www.impactscool.com) is a dedicated organization thinking about the future and discussing the impact of technologies on society.

TEN THINGS NOT TO BE MISSED

①**Creatures of 2050**
How have the species that inhabit our planet changed and what new creatures can be found? Robots, cyborgs, animal species that were believed to be extinct forever and new hybrids are at the order of the day.
To get there prepared see sections "The inhabitants" in Chapter 1 and "Animals and nature" in Chapter 2.

②**Space excursions**
One of the most popular destinations for visitors in 2050 is space. There are many agencies offering excursions and panoramic trips and the type of trip depends on the time available and the costs.
To choose the most suitable to satisfy your desires see subsections "Astrotourism" and "Romantic tours", both in Chapter 2.

③**Designed babies**
Among the things not to be missed is a visit to one of the laboratories that allow you to choose all DNA details of an unborn child. These are few and far between and not many allow tourists to visit.
For guidance on such a sensitive topic see subsection "'Designed' babies and the outsourcing of reproduction" in Chapter 1.

④**Synthetic–biological marriages**
You can't say you were in 2050 without witnessing this curious new custom. Many humans now decide to marry humanoid (human-like) robots.
For basic information see the subsection "Robots in love" in Chapter 1.

⑤**Functional food**
Tastes, shapes and colours are not lacking in the diet of 2050.
To discover foods with curative, preventive and cosmetic functions, see "Nutrition".

⑥**Urban farm**
The experience of a tour in one of the many city workshops where algae, vegetables and fruit are harvested using innovative methods is a must on a journey to a future that respects the Earth.
For a taste of tomorrow's kilometre zero dishes see subsection "2050 supermarkets" and following in Chapter 2.

⑦ Augmented sports
Attending a sporting event of the future, which includes robots, cyborgs, e-sport and augmented and virtual realities, certainly does not leave one disappointed.
To obtain a ticket, please refer to the section on "Sport and leisure time" in Chapter 2.

⑧ Souvenirs and shopping
Bags, shoes, notebooks and belts are not the same anymore. The material used to create them is produced in the laboratory from cells of the most varied animals on the planet. The most expensive are made from genuine synthetic human skin.
To get an idea of the new range of products on offer, see section "Seven deals not to be missed".

⑨ Tailor-made medicines
It is not surprising that, if necessary, before those in 2050 are prescribed any medication, they are subjected to a thorough DNA test and analysis of their personal parameters: there are almost no more general medicines.
To understand why tailor-made drugs are more effective see the section "Health" in Chapter 2.

⑩ Virtual dating
Between artificial intelligence-based matching systems and special virtual reality sets, distances no longer matter when it comes to finding your soulmate.
To experience a first date without leaving the house see subsection "Love, reproduction and relationships" in Chapter 1.

1 Snapshot of 2050

The inhabitants

Humans

Even if by 2050 the world's habitable surface area remains more or less the same as in 2020 (if it hasn't decreased), many more individuals will live on our planet: as Figure 2 shows, there are now more than 9.7 billion people on the Earth.[1]

It is important to note that more than half the *population growth* since 2017 is located in Africa, a continent where there has been an increase of 1.3 billion people, compared with an overall global increase of 2.2 billion.

Figure 2 Population distribution in 2050

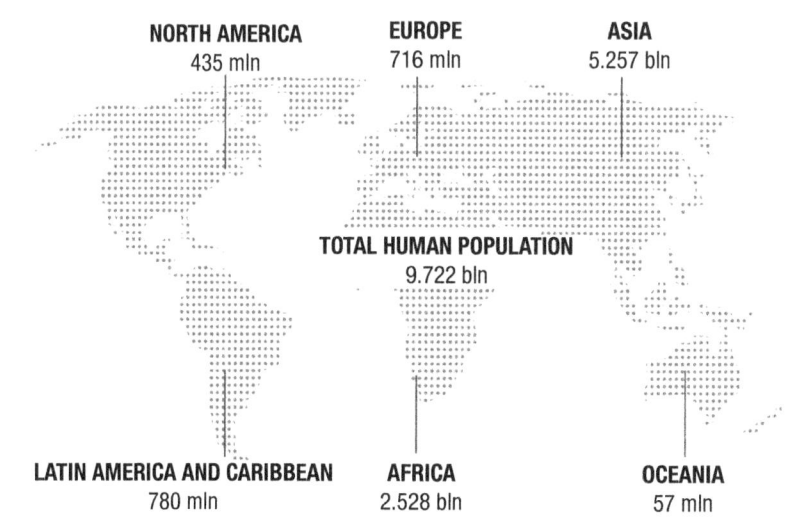

TOWARDS OVERPOPULATION?

If in 2050 there are almost 10 billion inhabitants, what should we expect by 2100? Will there be space on the planet for all human beings? What will the impacts on nature be? Is such growth sustainable? Such questions are not only legitimate but also crucially important. Let's try and find some answers.

1) How many of us are there?

According to the most accredited projections, the world population in 2100 will reach about 11.2 billion individuals. The demographic analysis has been elaborated considering the increase in births in developing countries, the prolongation of life expectancy, but also the decrease in births in those regions that see an increase in well-being and level of education.

2) Will there be enough room for everyone?

In 2011, the Per Square Mile project team, led by Tim de Chant, showed that in 2100, to accommodate all of humanity in a single city with the population density of New York in 2012, an area comparable to that of three American states will suffice.[2]

3) Will there be food for everyone?

Already in 2050 we are witnessing a revolution that raises concerns. But thanks to new agricultural techniques, systems for the production of animal proteins that reduce negative impacts on the planet and greater efficiency guaranteed by artificial intelligence and robotics, many problems can be overcome. Chapter 2, "Practical information", explains how.

4) So what are the problems with these statistics?

The issue is the increase in life expectancy and the relative ageing of the population. From a social point of view, support for the elderly becomes a priority, just as investment in research against ageing is crucial to ensuring a healthy and pleasant life even at an age beyond what we could dream of a few centuries ago. The cost of preventive care and medical interventions and their accessibility is a central issue in imagining a fair society, able to guarantee a minimum level of health for all its citizens.

Growth has particularly affected countries with already large populations or high birth rates, thus creating a strong concentration only in some regions of the world. In particular, half of the population growth took place in nine countries. In order of contribution: India, Nigeria, Democratic Republic of Congo, Pakistan, Ethiopia, United Republic of Tanzania, United States of America, Uganda and Indonesia. In many other countries, however, rates are falling. This is the case in Italy, where numbers have dropped from over 60 million inhabitants in 2018 to 55 million in 2050.[3]

Before proceeding, we must consider two important factors: first of all, *ease of movement* has vastly improved, so the measurement of the territorial distribution of populations must be looked at in perspective: many people live a nomadic life, without feeling the need to own a house or objects that are now not available in many parts of the world. Secondly, not all inhabitants are *properly human*, at least not in the conception widespread in 2020: some categories, such as those of cyborgs and mutants, are included in these calculations, but other subjects with citizenship, such as robots, are counted separately.

Let's start with these new categories.

Cyborgs

"We are, all of us, cyborgs in training": this is the start of an article from 2017 by Liat Clark,[4] a journalist and reporter who is an expert in technology, science, culture and politics. In fact, we already use tools such as computers, smartphones, wearable devices that increase our abilities, whether physical or cognitive.

CYBORG

The term *cyborg* derives from the contraction of *cybernetic organism* and, according to the classical definition, identifies a biological organism (for example, a human being) fused with an artificial element, also called an implantable device (for example, a chip, a pacemaker, a prosthesis).

Even more direct on what it means to be "cyborg in training" was Alexander Chislenko, Russian artificial intelligence theorist and active member of the transhumanist community until the year 2000, when he passed away (we will meet transhumanists again later and we will stop to better understand it). Chislenko described the present by stating that we are all *fyborgs*: hyper-connected "functional cyborgs" enhancing our capabilities with external technological tools, not directly grafted into our bodies. According to the scholar, however, the transition from the use of these external devices to similar, but integrated, devices will be very fast.

The inhabitants of the future are aware of this and, if you want to visit this faraway land, you should get used to it: in 2050 cyborgs are everywhere. However, you will not always identify them because their implants are often invisible and recharge themselves inside the body that houses them. A good way to distinguish between a human being and a transhuman is to try to guess his or her wealth: it is usually only the rich who can afford the most advanced implants. For this reason, movements are emerging that require states to guarantee the right to technological systems even to the most in need, ensuring a subsidy that allows everyone to keep up with the times and have the same opportunities.

CYBORGS TODAY

According to AFP, the French press agency, there are already over three thousand Swedish in 2020 who have implanted a chip in their hand: according to our definition they are therefore real cyborgs. These chips serve to open doors or make payments and also collect data, similar to the common fitness tracker we wear in the form of bracelets, watches or rings. At the moment the chips are very limited in their possibilities and the problem is minimal, but it is clear that they are hackable products and that in the future they could be at the centre of many cybersecurity crimes. This issue has already emerged in relation to devices such as pacemakers: increasingly connected and sophisticated, they are able to keep a person alive, but some researchers have revealed their vulnerabilities, warning manufacturers and patients.[5]

SPARTACUS: MENACE OR TOOL FOR FREEDOM?

Spartacus, a new Chinese company, launched a service on the market that immediately sparked a lot of controversy. Spartacus, in fact, offers anyone the possibility of obtaining a free brain implant to increase their cognitive abilities. In exchange for this service, the beneficiaries are required to watch at least three advertisements every hour, transmitted through special retinal lenses.

The famous cyborg actor J.J. Beta has welcomed the news: Spartacus, in his view, allows a large number of less well-off people to access the latest development in neurotechnologies. His opponents, however, consider the obligation to watch advertisements questionable. They also argue that the service should be free of charge and guaranteed by the state.

Mutants

Less common than cyborgs are those who, borrowing a term from science fiction, can be called *mutants*. These individuals have modified DNA that can differ from that of other human beings because of genetic mutations that are often the result of micro- and macro-interventions in genetic editing, carried out by as a result of treatments for disease, prevention of hereditary anomalies or, although still rarely, the dictates of fashion. There are those, for example, who try to use editing to acquire typical capabilities of some animals, such as seeing in the dark or breathing underwater. This type of operation obviously entails strong moral implications, and for this reason its use has given rise to numerous controversies.

GENETIC EDITING TODAY

Depending on the model, a kit for gene editing at home costs between $80 and $650 and can easily be purchased online. We are talking about the genetic control kits using the CRISPR-CAS9 technique,[6] designed for amateur use. They allow bacteria to be manipulated, hybrids to be created, animals and humans to be modified. They are sold by The Odin, a company founded by Josiah Zayner, a member of the biohacker movement.

> Biohacking is a recent achievement and is based on the assumption that if experimentation were more easily available, scientific progress could increase significantly. This unsupervised technique, however, can present some risks. According to Dr Maria Cristina Magli, in an interview to *Corriere della Sera*,[7] those who attempt this could make accidental changes to DNA which we do not know are integrated into the system, while completely ignoring the protocols that are followed in the laboratories could create pollution or uncontrolled consequences, such as releasing modified bacteria into the environment, allowing them to multiply. For the time being, there are no laws on this subject except in Germany, where it has been established that anyone who conducts genetic experiments outside the specified areas is liable to a fine of up to €50,000 and imprisonment for up to three years.

Advanced humans

In 2050, even those who, by choice or necessity, have remained completely human have a mind different from the inhabitants of 2020. The "average" human being is initiated into a series of changes, due to the environment and society, which influence his or her physical and aesthetic appearance. In particular, we can see two main trends: the size of the male reproductive organs is decreasing, due to the effect of widespread well-being (it is no longer necessary to reproduce at the same rate as in the past and infant mortality is declining), and also the shape of the brain is changing, reducing, overall, its size. Don't worry, however, all this does not mean that the inhabitants of the future will be less intelligent, but that they will use the brain in a different way compared to us: the parts of the brain used in situations that threaten survival in wild environments, parts on which depend, for example, the functional aggressiveness of hunting and which are already in decline in our days, following a trend that has lasted ten thousand years, will shrink. The frontal part of the brain, on the contrary, is destined to develop, essentially, that which is necessary for reading, writing and understanding: all the activities, especially the last one, necessary for being successful from the social point of view and, therefore, for surviving in the future. Nature, as we know, accentuates and selects the winning characters.

In 2050, however, these changes will not yet be fully apparent, but an increasingly proactive trend will be noticeable as people will be forced to become more and more competitive in the new context as a result of social pressure.

Superhumans

The technology, science, genetics and medicine of 2050 are working hard as instruments of the same orchestra, directed towards a single, great and ancient goal: the extension of human life. Humanity has always dreamed of overcoming the natural limits imposed on all forms of life and in 2050 there is a swarm of solutions, tests, experiments and studies that move in this direction.

Although it is not yet possible to really think of an immortal being, these solutions seeking to enhance human capabilities and push beyond the limits of the level of health of individuals are initiating the laboratory construction of real superhumans.

Anyone who advocates the need for human beings to transcend nature in one or more of these ways is called a transhumanist. In the following paragraphs we will delve into many of the solutions that are undergoing testing and analysis, but an initial glance, together with that provided by Figure 3, may be useful to get a first idea.

Figure 3 The dream of transhumans to create a superhuman

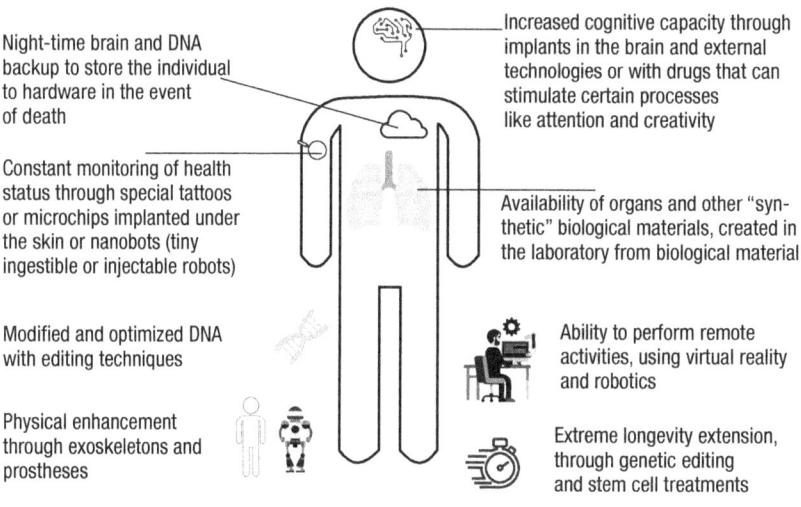

Night-time brain and DNA backup to store the individual to hardware in the event of death

Constant monitoring of health status through special tattoos or microchips implanted under the skin or nanobots (tiny ingestible or injectable robots)

Modified and optimized DNA with editing techniques

Physical enhancement through exoskeletons and prostheses

Increased cognitive capacity through implants in the brain and external technologies or with drugs that can stimulate certain processes like attention and creativity

Availability of organs and other "synthetic" biological materials, created in the laboratory from biological material

Ability to perform remote activities, using virtual reality and robotics

Extreme longevity extension, through genetic editing and stem cell treatments

Humanoid robots and other life companions

Walking the streets of 2050 we meet many creatures, more or less identical with humans. We can have a chat with them, they have varied jobs and, sometimes, they can deceive us by looking like members of our species. But beware: robots with artificial intelligence can be concealed behind the human aspect.

In some countries, in order not to create confusion, it is mandatory to be clear about one's nature; in others, however, this obligation is seen as a discriminatory act and asking someone if they are a robot is considered rude. It is therefore necessary to find out more about the regulations in force in the countries you are visiting, so as not to run into problems with the law. Consider that in 2050 the number of service robots (i.e. excluding industrial robots) is one robot per inhabitant globally and that in 2070 the ratio is expected to grow to ten robots per inhabitant (Figure 4).[8]

Figure 4 Human–robot ratio in 2050 and 2070: How many service robots per inhabitant?

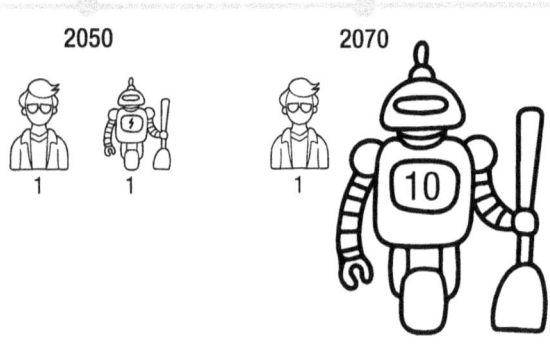

In 2050 it is normal for most wealthy people to have at least one personal robot dedicated to supporting them in various activities. These artificial intelligence automatons take care of the house (coordinating domestic robots), people's children, animals and gardens; they organize people's agendas and personal and business appointments, provide companionship and perform hundreds of other functions.

Many of these robots with artificial intelligence are also used as social support for people with psychological problems, disabilities or serious illnesses, and for that part of the population that has passed the age of 65. Of the more than 9 billion people living on the planet in 2050, about 2 billion have already turned 60, compared to just under 1 billion in 2018. In 2050, in more than thirty-six countries in the world in Europe, Asia and Latin America, the ratio between those who are under 65 and those who are older has fallen below two: that is to say, for every person over 65, there are fewer than two younger people.

It should be noted that while in 2018 the only countries in which for every person under 25 there was one who was over 65 were Italy and Japan, in 2050 this ratio is valid for thirty-six countries and the record is held by Portugal, with over 3 million over 65, against only about 1.1 million under 25 (Figure 5 shows a comparison between 2018 and 2050 of the population under 25 and over 65).[9]

The presence of many robots of all types that offer assistance to the segment of the population over 60 years of age will not seem strange, therefore. However, there are few countries that have adopted a policy of support for their elderly citizens and that grant the use of these expensive tools free of charge.

Figure 5 Percentage of population under 25 and over 65 compared (2018/2050)

	0–25			> 60	
	number of individuals	% country		number of individuals	% country
2018	1,527,649	20%		990,499	7%
2025	1,669,171	17%		2,080,459	21%

Source: Elaboration on United Nations data, *World Population Prospects*, 2017.

Inhabited places

City or countryside? In 2050, around 68 per cent of the population live permanently in urban centres. To understand the extent of the phenomena – just think that one hundred years earlier, in 1950, the proportion was reversed: only 30 per cent of the global population lived in cities (in 2018 this percentage is around 55 per cent).[10]

About 3.1 billion people in 2050 live in rural areas, but the important data to consider is that, of these, 10 per cent are distributed between India (almost 900 million individuals) and China (just under 600 million), and 90 per cent of this population is in Africa and the rest of Asia (Figure 6).

Figure 6 Proportion between rural and urban population: evolution 1950–2050

1950	2018	2050
Urban population 30%	Urban population 55%	Urban population 68%
Rural population 70%	Rural population 45%	Rural population 32%

Source: Elaboration on United Nations data, *World Urbanization Prospects*, 2018.

But what are the cities of 2050 like? Some are smart cities, others are populated as if they were entire nations. Let's take a closer look at them.

Megacities

A megacity is a city with more than 10 million inhabitants. In 2050 the main megacities, in order of size, are: Mumbai (India), Delhi (India), Dhaka (Bangladesh), Kinshasa (Democratic Republic of Congo), Kolkata (India) (Figure 7).[11]

Figure 7 The ten most populated megacities in 2050 (million inhabitants)

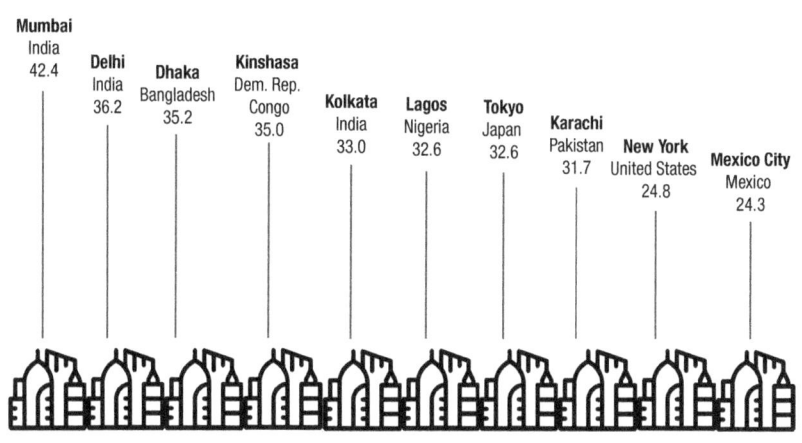

Source: Elaboration of data from D. Hoornweg and K. Pope, *Socioeconomic Pathways and Regional Distribution of the World's 101 Largest Cities*, 2014.

What is life like in a megacity? The answer is not univocal and depends on the level of overall well-being in which the city itself has developed and on the urban philosophy followed by the builders. Asian megacities, for example, tend to be modern, globalized and rich, while African megacities, such as Lagos in Niger, are often crowded, degraded and dangerous, as they have developed in unstable political situations and with large social gaps. In Lagos two thirds of the districts are poor and unhealthy.

If you decide to visit any of them, remember that the climate in these urban agglomerations is on average much warmer than in the past: up to four or five degrees warmer than in 1950 in large cities (we will return to this aspect in Figure 13 in Chapter 2).

An example of a megacity that is very liveable for its inhabitants is Tokyo, where you live in what we could call "neighbourhoods": even though it is built around a centre, the city is made up of many small "villages" in which the citizen could easily spend the whole day without ever moving from one area to another. Each district is not only equipped with all services, but also with relaxation and meeting areas for its inhabitants, which encourages the social interaction typical of small towns.

Smart cities

Smart cities are designed and planned on the basis of completely new infrastructures, mobility and public services. These urban centres take advantage of technological advances to optimize energy efficiency, mobility, pollution control, green areas and, ultimately, their own habitability. Advanced artificial intelligence algorithms analyse the data collected by millions of sensors and networked objects (cars, public transport, citizens' habits, events and demonstrations, health facilities, public offices), generating information that makes the city efficient and minimizes environmental impacts.

In the most modern smart cities you can admire buildings, bridges and other infrastructure printed in 3D with a significant reduction in time and construction costs.

An example of a smart city to visit in 2050 is Belmont, for several years the smartest city on the planet. Sustainable and technologically advanced, Belmont (not yet in existence in 2020) is located in the Arizona desert and was founded by Bill Gates and his company Mt. Lemmon Holdings. More than 80,000 inhabitants, 15 square kilometres of commercial and industrial space, 14 square kilometres of open space and 2 whole kilometres dedicated to public education: real ecosystems – but smart – the first to use new technologies and opportunities – Belmont exploited the possibility of building and designing a city from scratch in the early 21st century.

If you have time, don't miss the cities built in the Arab Emirates and China. They, too, are among the first smart cities on the planet, and have set a new standard in the choice of the most extravagant materials and architectural styles.

Space communities

Since the year 2000, some human beings have been living in space. We are referring to the inhabitants of the Orbital Station. What happens in 2050, however, is very different. These are not temporary missions in contact with the Earth, but real colonizations of other celestial bodies. The Moon, for example, is a transit and supply hub, with a community of about two thousand people,[12] who, although still depending on our planet for food and much more (they have not yet found a way to be totally sustainable), live on the only natural satellite of the Earth. The mission to Mars sponsored by Elon Musk is famous.[13] Already in 2016 he was planning to bring about 1 million people to live on the Red Planet (more attractive than the Moon) starting from 2030; however, its enterprise has only succeeded in part, and the number of people living on Mars in 2050 is about 20,000,[14] mostly scientists, researchers, engineers and, to a lesser extent, explorers.

Communication between space communities and the Earth is subject to a two-minute delay, because of the limits of the speed of light, and it is possible for Earthlings to follow such communities' events and life through shows, videos and stories in augmented and virtual reality. We will go into more detail about space tourism excursions by talking about astrotourism in the section "Sport and leisure time" in Chapter 2.

Culture

Languages

One thing that has not changed in 2050 compared to 2018 is the classification of the most globally spoken languages (Figure 8). The record is still held, even in 2050, by Mandarin Chinese, followed by Spanish, English, Arabic and Hindi. The proportions have changed a little, with an increase in Arabic and Hindi,[15] and, even though it has not arrived at the top, French has climbed the charts, driven by the increase in population in French-speaking African countries.

Figure 8 Ranking of the most spoken languages in the world (first language) in 2018

Mandarin Chinese	1.299 mln
Spanish	442 mln
English	378 mln
Arabic	315 mln
Hindi	269 mln

Source: Elaboration of data from Statista, *The most spoken languages worldwide* (native speakers in millions), https://www.statista.com, 2018.

Religions

In 2050, considering the increase in population by geographical and cultural area, clear data shows that the Islamic religion has equalled the Christian religion in percentage and thus is practised by a third of the world population. The other confessions, on the other hand, have decreased their percentage weight, even though the number of faithful has increased (Table 1).[16]

Table 1 Percentage weight of world population of religions in 2050

	% of population in 2010	% of population in 2050	Delta
Christians	31.40%	31.35%	–0.05%
Muslims	23.20%	29.67%	6.47%
Atheists	16.40%	13.22%	–3.18%
Hindus	15.00%	14.87%	–0.13%
Buddhists	7.10%	5.22%	–1.88%
Popular religions	5.90%	4.83%	–1.07%
Other	0.80%	0.66%	–0.14%
Jews	0.20%	0.17%	–0.03%

Source: Pew Research Center, *The Future of World Religions: Population Growth Projections, 2010–2050*, 2015.

Alongside the religions and orientations that we know of in 2020, new pseudo-religious movements, which we can call *techno-religions*, were born and are spreading in 2050, strongly influenced by technology and its advancements.

As Yuval Noah Harari explains in his *Homo Deus*,[17] two new macro-trends have developed: *techno-humanism* and *data religion*. The first one believes that Homo sapiens no longer have any sense of existence as we know it and that are destined to evolve into new artificially created forms. The latter, on the other hand, is based on the assumption that humans must pass the baton to new non-biological entities (hardware and servers, for example) capable of processing and managing data faster, more comprehensively and more efficiently than humans themselves.

The alphabet of the new generations

When we talk about generations, we mean groups of individuals shaped by the culture at the period of their birth and by the global events of the society in which they grew up.

The Baby Boomers, for example, are the first to have adopted the initial forms of information technology and their youth was marked by the advent of television; the so-called Generation X was marked instead, in its growth, by the advent of personal computing. Generation Y (the Millennials), on the other hand, grew up in the midst of the digital revolution.

Once the letters of the Latin alphabet were completed with Generation Z, which was born in the midst of the spread of the Internet, three new generations made their entrance into our society, inaugurating the Greek alphabet: the Alpha, the Beta and the Gamma. The year 2050 is their kingdom (Figure 9).

Before proceeding, however, let's take a brief look at the dates of birth in which we can place the different generations (Figure 10).

Figure 9 Breakdown of population by generation in 2050

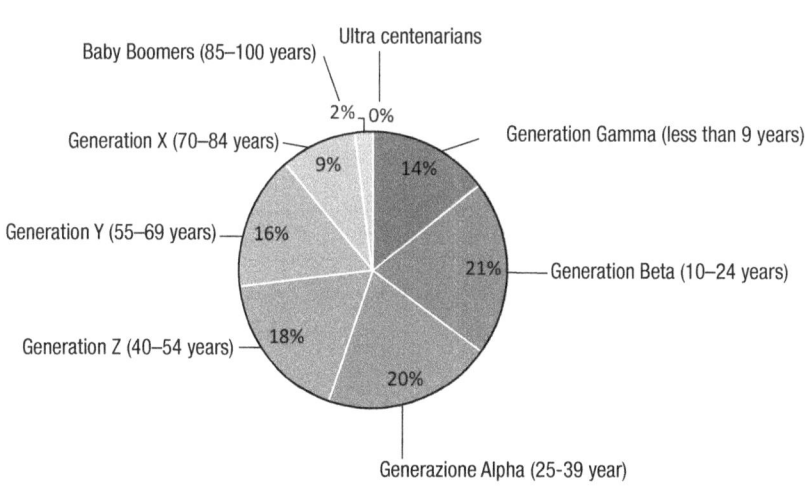

Source: Elaboration on United Nations data, *World Population Prospects*, 2017.

Figure 10 The alphabet of generations (by year of birth)

Baby Boomers	1945–1965
Generation X	1965–1980
Generation Y	1980–1995
Generation Z	1995–2010
Generation Alpha	2010–2025
Generation Beta	2025–2040
Generation Gamma	2040 and up

In 2050, the workforce is mainly made up of Generations Y, Z, Alpha and Beta, while the Generation Gamma is still too young. In particular, the Generation Alpha has entered the labour market, together with the very first Beta representatives.

Let us therefore try to reflect on this. The comparison between Generations X and Y is mainly based on cultural factors linked to historical events and symbolic objects and concepts such as MTV and the iPhone, respectively. The passage to the generations from Z onwards, on the other hand, is more discontinuous due to the effects of technology. For millennia, our brains have developed based on simulations derived from physical reality. Since the twenty-first century, however, these new generations have found themselves immersed, from an early age, in numerous forms of reality (digital, virtual, augmented) that are aimed at creating a constantly connected world, capable of merging digital and physical environments into a new, unique, complex reality. The brains of these generations, therefore, have necessarily evolved, as a result of the new stimuli received. And so, more and more people's brains have been developed, focusing on very specific skills and a high level of specialization, with better results in visual skills and in multitasking, and with improved hand–eye coordination.[18]

The children of the Generations Alpha and Beta were impacted by the *internet of toys*: a series of educational games with network connections, able to incorporate intelligent algorithms and to integrate with voice commands as if they were human beings. While the Generation Beta has grown up in a world where much of its education has been dedicated to understanding technologies, their risks and the best way to use them, Generation Alpha, on the other hand, has not had this opportunity and has found itself facing numerous privacy and security issues, learning to understand these concepts alone. Moreover, if reality has become more complex and has united digital, virtual and physical worlds in a single frame, in the digital world these generations preserve different personalities and devote a lot of time to the management of their own "brand" online, virtual and augmented.

As we shall see, this is increasingly central in social interactions. With all these changes, the generational differences that characterize 2050 are easily imaginable. But don't worry, in order to facilitate the ability of communication between members of different generations, there are artificial intelligence systems, which guarantee simultaneous translation and allow people who are very distant from each other to understand each other, as if they were speaking different languages.

Anthropocene

The year 2050 is the first century of a new geological era, which we are already inhabitants of in 2020. This is an era characterized by the very strong impact of technology and people on nature: the Anthropocene.[19]

For the first time in history, the most critical factors influencing our destiny are determined by human beings and the technology that they produce and create. Unlike the Holocene, the previous geological era, which lasted 11,700 years, the impact of humans on the Earth has increased to a disproportionate degree. To give us an idea, consider that in 2017 we were already using 50 per cent of the land available to produce food, build cities, roads and mines, we used 40 per cent of the planet's net production and we controlled three-quarters of the freshwater resources.

Human beings have become the most widespread animal of note on the planet and, with their activities, they threaten to kill about one fifth of the other existing species.[20]

THE EFFECTS OF HUMANITY ON PLANET EARTH

A study published by *Nature* in 2018 highlighted the extent of the impact of human beings on the planet.[21] Wildlife is simply going away. With the exception of Antarctica, only 23 per cent of the land and 13 per cent of the oceans remain free from harmful anthropogenic activities. To understand the extent of the impact, let's consider that a century earlier the percentage of land that had emerged but not been exploited by man was 85 per cent. In 2050, nature is in the hands of only five countries: Australia, Russia, Canada, the USA (Alaska) and Brazil are responsible for 70 per cent of the areas to be protected.
A World Wildlife Fund (WWF) report released more or less at the same time as *Nature's* article shows how the ongoing changes affect biodiversity: in the fifty years preceding 2018, 60 per cent of the vertebrate population was lost.[22] For this reason, the negotiation of treaties for the protection of the planet has already begun, such as the Marine Biodiversity Treaty for the protection of the oceans,[23] or the initiatives of the Antarctic Ocean Commission (CCAMLR),[24] which proposes to create a protected area of 2 million square metres, the largest on our planet, in the Antarctic itself.

If we think about the impacts of human beings, we cannot but speak about the enormous amount of waste that invades our planet and space. Like all ecosystems, the Earth works by input and output: the input is the energy that activates the processes, the output is the waste that results.

An ecosystem is sustainable if it is able to activate its processes by disposing of waste efficiently in a zero-sum game, recycling waste so that it produces energy in turn. In 2050, the inhabitants of the Earth are making enormous efforts to make the system sustainable, so that the creation of waste does not have negative impact. It is, however, a challenge that requires global collaboration and the ability to accurately assess the impacts of new technologies that are continuously being developed.

Geoengineering

In 2050, there is heated discussion about the potential of geoengineering and its impacts. Geoengineering is the ability to deliberately manipulate the atmosphere to achieve climate change over the entire planet. The proposals made over time, from as early as the 1980s, are extremely varied, from installing a giant deflector in space, to lifting 50,000 sails capable of blocking 1 per cent of the sun's rays, to doing the same but with millions of tiny structures, more efficient in terms of cost and feasibility. There are also scientists who suggest solutions that risk being irreversible, such as "sowing" iron in the oceans to increase the growth of plankton, injecting sulphur compounds into the stratosphere to form a kind of shield to reflect part of the sun's rays, or removing carbon dioxide from the atmosphere through special towers. By 2050 these techniques had already been tested many times and their potential was well known. However, the impacts of these projects in the medium and long term are not yet clear.

The fact is that anyone who decides to proceed with such experiments might change the whole planet: if any go wrong, huge natural disasters will result. For this to happen, all countries and their governments need to agree and act in unison and, above all, to know in detail what the effects may be, including the undesirable ones. In the meantime, there are those who support the need to carry out new tests, perhaps trying to intervene, with much more invasive systems, on other planets of the Solar System to make them habitable, artificially creating an atmosphere suitable for the life of human beings (later, speaking of Mars, we will also take advantage of some of these projects, which go by the name of *terraforming*).

GEOENGINEERING

The first geoengineering experiments date back to 2017, in Arizona, when a group of Harvard researchers tried for the first time to verify if what had been theorized until then was feasible in reality. In particular, the first experiments were aimed at understanding which was the right molecule to "spray" into the atmosphere to shield the sun's rays.

The political landscape

The political and institutional landscape of 2050 is surprising for a traveller arriving from 2020, accustomed to completely different forms of governance and systems, the result of an evolution that began in ancient Greece and culminated with the birth of the nation states.

In 2050, under the pressure of the changes of the last decades, citizens decided to try to restart from scratch, creating a new system of government capable of keeping up with the times in an increasingly complex and radically different world from that in which Aristotle, Machiavelli, Montesquieu, Rousseau, Tocqueville and many of the thinkers who contributed, with their theories, to creating the forms of government in use in the twenty-first century lived.

The reality of 2050 is strongly influenced by the new technologies, first and foremost the Internet, and all institutions cannot fail to take this into account, as they are the repositories of the powers to manage the most important aspects of society: education, rights, laws, defence, economics, reforms and so on.

It is useful to make a premise because, if the means and the ways have changed, the logics that make up the pillar of the concept of the form of government and that of its institutions have remained the same. Without delving into theories on possible forms of government, we can, however, agree upon the common points of those which foresee, albeit to different strengths and degrees, the participation of each adult citizen in public decisions. The logic is simple: as it is not possible to manage a decision-making process that involves everyone, people can choose by voting for a limited number of people who are able to represent their interests and are suitable for managing the municipality. Depending on the system, the ratio of vote to person is more or less direct. The choice, when we vote, falls (or should fall) on the candidates who most seem to embody our values and, consequently, our ideas. That is, people who can defend the rights that we believe to be fundamental not only for us, but for all of us. How is the voting preference expressed? In 2020, we still voted for candidates physically situated in dedicated places (seats) that were suitably controlled and, therefore, considered official: a process that took place in a historical moment in which the tools available to obtain an official and secure vote were limited to paper and pen (or rather, a copying pencil, given that at that time ballpoint pens did not yet exist). By 2050, however, the Internet, quantum computers, blockchain technology, artificial intelligence algorithms, innovative methods for measuring online reputation, social networks and virtual aggregation systems have revolutionized both the way of thinking about a country's government and the possibilities of expressing one's own opinions. It is a continuation of a path that began in the first decades of the millennium: just think of the events that have changed the world (the Arab Spring, to name but one), spread all over the Internet, Twitter and Facebook; or the political campaigns that play out on social networks and are guided by artificial intelligence algorithms and the analysis of huge amounts of data.

PLATFORMS FOR ACTIVE CITIZENS

Numerous online platforms, active on political and social issues, show us how, in 2020, new tools for social and political engagement already exist.
Think, for example, of all the non-profit areas on crowdfunding platforms like Indiegogo and Kickstarter, or on dedicated platforms such as GoFundMe, GiveForward, Fundly, Razoo and Causes.
There are also several sites that specialize in collecting signatures for online petitions, such as Change.org, which aim to appeal to the public on a variety of topics.

The revolution of instruments

In 2050 many of the ideas and experiments were inspired by the successes (and mistakes) of all those groups that, in the early 2000s, tried to change their models of government. In the future, for example, flat forms such as DemocracyOS, created in Argentina by a team of supporters, programmers, students and activists led by Pia Mancini,[25] are used. It is one of the first models of open source democracy,[26] based on free, easy-to-use software that allows citizens to stay informed, participate in debates and make their voices heard by governments. Other very interesting cases are the open source software Liquid Feedback, which provides a valuable collaboration tool to support democracy and the need to make group decisions, and the Parliament Watch platform,[27] which creates a direct link between deputies and citizens, promoting transparency and participation.

The keyword of 2050 is experimentation. Get ready to discover, then, new models of government. In order to understand what is happening in this surprising destination, we are first of all concentrating on the tools to exercise the right to vote.

THE CASE OF ESTONIA

The first online voting experiments date back to 2012, when the possibility of voting via the Internet was introduced in Estonia, with the result that in the parliamentary elections of 1 March 2015, more than a third of those entitled to vote expressed themselves online. Most of them were - as expected - young people voting for the first time. The system introduced by Estonia was very simple: it was based on a €50 reader and the use of an electronic identity card (equipped with a microchip); a set of passwords protected the identity of the voter and controlled the number of votes per person, as well as ensuring the security and secrecy of the vote itself.

In order to understand the economic advantage of such a solution, it was estimated that the 2013 elections in Italy cost, in terms of personnel, polling station management, polls and organization in general, about 400 million euros. A study held in UK comparing the cost of an online voting system and a traditional one showed that online could reach a 15% cost cut for an average national election.[28]

In 2050, the use of technology to express voting preferences is taken for granted: the participation of citizens in the choices of their country therefore has a cost close to zero. The blockchain and other decriminalized systems guarantee a safe, secret and immediate vote, without the need for third parties to check that the process takes place correctly. Citizens can be consulted directly and quickly, so that it is considered normal to express one's opinion at least once a week, starting from adulthood. Voting takes place through special apps, installed on wearable devices and more or less integrated with the body, which interact with the certified digital identity of each citizen.

CROWDSOURCING THE LAW

Taiwan is experimenting with using the vTaiwan[29] platform to create a participatory legislative process. Laws are discussed online by citizens, organizations, experts and elected representatives. The government then uses the suggestions, which come freely from the platform, as recommendations. It is certainly difficult to imagine that, once citizens have been mobilized to engage in this process, parliamentarians will not seek consensus by showing that they are listening to the preferences of the majority. Will it work?

Votes by influence

In some countries of 2050, so-called "democracy by influence" has established itself. To understand what is meant by this expression, try to imagine having to give a camera to a friend who is passionate about photography. You understand little or nothing about photography but you want to buy the best product for him. Let's assume we are in 1997; you have two options: buy a specialized magazine and hope to find useful information, or go to a camera shop, describe your friend and the type of photographs he loves to take, and get advice from a salesman. In the latter case, you do not personally know who will advise you, but you know that it is usual to seek advice in such a way and that the company has a good reputation, which you trust. Let's take a step forward to 2020: you have another possibility – which will most likely be the one you choose – namely to go online and visit specialist websites to garner information and read reviews. You can also take a peek at your friend's social profile: he will certainly have published photos taken by him, images of his camera and, in the best-case scenario, will have mentioned his favourite brand.

In 2050, things are even easier. Intelligent algorithms could tell us who is the ideal person to ask for advice on the camera to give to our friend. Thanks to a rating system that assesses all social activities, reviews and skills and the reliability of people in certain areas, the inhabitants of 2050 can trace the best experts on any subject in a few moments.

Let's take this a step further: let's assume that in our country there is a need to approve a regulation that has strong repercussions on the photography market. If we were in one of the countries of the future where this curious (and discussed) form of democracy has developed, there would be two choices: the citizen can study the information him/herself to try to decide how to vote, or he/she can identify the person who has the most suitable expertise to make this decision and with whom, at the same time, he/she shares basic values and a vision of the world. At this point, the system allows you to assign your vote to the person of your choice; when the time comes to vote, then, the vote of this person will be worth double, while the citizen who delegated his/her vote will not vote. The voting method applies to all, of course, and this means that, depending on the vote, a citizen may be awarded one or more votes or may choose to assign their vote to another. In 2050, this system is, however, leading to scandals and discussions at the global level, since there is a clear risk of concentrating decision-making power in the hands of a few, without a real guarantee of transparency in the definition of the rating and the rate of influence. The states that have adopted this system are therefore facing the difficult challenge of ensuring that it is truly sustainable, safe, transparent and fair in the medium and long term.

Ratings and parameters

Some governments have gone even further and are using a rating system to determine citizens' preferential access to social and health services, verifying their trustworthiness, transparency and values considered important to ensure the construction of a peaceful and prosperous society, and rewarding those with the best score.

Regardless of the form of government, this rating system is used, with different rules, by almost all countries. Each country applies various algorithms for calculating the personal rating of cities; in some cases these algorithms are transparent and certified, in others they are kept secret.

The most common parameters for rating measurements are trust, impact and happiness creation, and these are measurable through complex artificial intelligence algorithms that analyse huge amounts of data from wearable devices, social networks, brand databases, institutions and more. The systems are increasingly fine-tuning themselves and are able to calculate each parameter accurately.

These include:

- *Trust*: a fundamental parameter for human interaction since the time of Homo sapiens, in 2050 it was measured with great precision thanks to the traceability of every personal detail and the reviews

received from other citizens. This parameter is considered so clear and certain that now almost all transactions and interactions between citizens are decentralized and pass through platforms that do not provide for the presence of intermediaries. Some examples of transactions that take place in this way are: the sale or rental, even for just one day, of an apartment or office; the transfer of rights to an object to be printed in 3D; the execution of a will; the making of a donation (we will also come back to this in terms of currency).
- *Impact*: thanks to the interaction of augmented reality and artificial intelligence, the concept of impact can be used as a yardstick for any decision. The 2050 passenger compartments can choose the best means of transport by which they can be used, give the restaurant the dish to be ordered and the actions to be taken, assessing the impact that their choice will have in a given period of time both on themselves and on others. Artificial intelligence performs the calculation and the autonomous reality shows it in an immersive and realistic way, thus influencing the actions of citizens. This also makes it possible to measure, according to the parameters chosen by the countries that use the system, the amount of happiness that each citizen is able to generate in others and, therefore, in society.
- *Creation of happiness*: according to the supporters of this system, when the rate of reliability and the impact that each citizen has on him/herself, others and, more generally, on society have been established, it becomes easy to calculate the amount of happiness that each citizen can create around him/herself and the persons with whom he or she interacts.

The idea of creating a social structure based on trust and the use of technology is undoubtedly fascinating. However, there are several aspects to consider when evaluating this rating system.

First of all, there is the problem of complexity. In 2020, we are all already living more than one reality and have more than one personality. Far from having a transparent representation of what we are in physical reality, new realities to "be someone else" is the order of the day: social networks, communities and virtual realities create new images of us, with the effect of multiplying our imaginary "self" and the degrees of reality in which we operate. Even before the Internet we lived in different degrees of reality: dreams, experience, imagination, recurrence and so on, all levels in which our brain subjects us to different experiences. In the present, realities have multiplied and this also applies to our personalities, which do not always reflect those in the physical world.

A JUMP INTO THE PRESENT: THE CHINESE SOCIAL CREDIT SYSTEM

For those who are on their way to 2050 from 2020, the idea of a citizens' rating system might sound familiar, since it was in that very period in history that the concept began to spread, thanks to an episode of the successful television series Black Mirror aired on Netflix, and then, on terrestrial TV, in China.[30]

The Chinese case is particularly important because it allows one to grasp the different possible uses of the technologies mentioned in this chapter: blockchain, artificial intelligence, quantum computers, data collection of all kinds, including those relating to health and DNA. Put all these things together and put them in the hands of a powerful regime: you will have all the ingredients for possible future dystopias, dreadful beyond imagination. In particular, when we talk about artificial intelligence, in 2020 the race (renamed in 2050 the Second Cold War) sees two main actors competing: USA and China. These two powers are attracting the best talents, building cloud systems and collecting huge datasets: elements needed for global leadership in artificial intelligence. Both are aware of the fact that artificial intelligence represents a huge competitive advantage, not only in the development of autonomous weapons and systems to support defence (we will address the subject in the pages dedicated to "War and technology") but also in economic terms. While the USA is leaving room for private businesses linked to the exploitation of citizens' data, aiming at economic growth, China sees artificial intelligence as a tool for the control and management of citizens and relies on government applications such as the Social Credit System (SCS). This Chinese rating system, mandatory for all Chinese citizens since 2020, is a tool for assessing the reliability of citizens, institutions and companies, based on the observation of their online behaviour. It takes into account parameters such as:

- credit history (e.g. payments of bills or telephone accounts)
- the ability to fulfil one's contractual obligations
- buying habits
- personal information
- online friends and comments posted on social media.

Do you think that these are dystopian perspectives that transform transparency and sincerity into a nightmare as in *Black Mirror* or in the book *The Circle*?[31] Come and visit the countries in 2050 and judge for yourself.

But how do you assess a person's reliability? In which area should it be assessed? And which of the many personalities we embody should be taken into account? To try to answer these questions, let's analyse how the interaction between individual and reality works through the brain.

It should be noted that we still know very little about this fascinating organ. What we know with sufficient certainty is that it makes continuous predictions about the behaviour of others, basing its projections on all available information. This is why anthropologists argue that forms of social interaction such as gossip, which allow us to significantly increase the information available to us about other people, have always played an essential role in the development of communities of human beings that are increasingly numerous and able to collaborate with each other. The more I know about the situation in front of me, the easier it is for me to try to predict what might happen. Think about it: when we are faced with someone who seems not to follow our canons and our rules of reasoning, whether they are members of a community with cultural characteristics very different from ours, animals or people who are mentally ill, our instinctive reactions are fear and suspicion.

Let's get back to the forecasts made by our brain. This is what happens: the brain continuously creates images and explanations that inform us on how the future might unfold and, therefore, the behaviour of others around us. At this point, the body and the senses do an important job of verifying what is imagined and predicted by the brain and, through the inputs collected from the surrounding world, confirm or deny these predictions. It is a complex system that has developed over millennia of evolution and is not governed by pure rationality, but combines instinct, experience and calculation.

Can an artificial rating system really match this complex activity of the human brain? What it is able to do, at first glance, may seem even more evolved than our instinct because, in addition to managing a quantity of data that goes beyond our cognitive abilities, it is able to keep track of feedback from other human beings and of data and information.

The new realities that we frequent and that mirror our different virtual, digital and augmented personalities are scattered throughout the world more widely than we could be in person. However, we cannot fail to ask ourselves how these rating systems activate the process of assessing reliability, which personalities and realities they should take into account, and with what weight. Can an algorithm really replicate or exceed the capabilities of our brains in this area?

The secret of the process that we humans activate does not – or at least does not only – reside in the amount of data available. The real marvel is the way we evaluate and analyse such data: our brain works differently to an artificial intelligence algorithm. First of all, the algorithms don't forget: they don't give second chances to anyone, but we (fortunately) do. Moreover, they are created to apply the rules sequentially, without exception; they do not have the human common sense on the basis of which our society accepts that, from time to time, some rules are broken (we will resume these reinterpretations when dealing with the subject of transport, particularly with reference to the functioning of self-driving cars). In the face of all these variables, it is inevitable that the adoption of rating systems and influence ratings will be accompanied by doubts and controversy.

The most critical argue that these systems jeopardize the freedom of citizens and end up putting enormous power in the hands of a few, rewarding people who, having the economic opportunity, invest more than others and manage to obtain the influence and visibility necessary to convince citizens to delegate their vote to them. Others criticize the decision to leave to a small group of people the choice of how to program the algorithms, establishing what should be evaluated, whether there are things to delete and how, what is false or true, how reliable people are and, ultimately, their access to social services. The predecessor of algorithms, on the other hand, our brain, has always been in the hands of a complex society, made up of millions of people and shaped by thousands of years of evolution.

Artificial "dictators"

Some countries are experimenting with a new form of government, based entirely on artificial intelligence. Citizens have elected an electronic super brain as Head of State and all other members of the government have become mere executors of what is decided by the algorithm. In these countries, citizens do not express single votes or preferences, but are obliged, from birth and throughout their lives, to provide data and information to the algorithm, which, in this way, can make decisions based on complete and reliable indications.

Artificial intelligence is considered superior in all respects to human beings, able to protect the common good,[32] and able to take the most correct decisions for society in the legislative, economic and social spheres. Therefore, there are software programs that play the role of judge or managing director.

However, given the high concentration of these technologies in the hands of a few multinational companies, which have by now become very powerful, it often happens that algorithms from different countries take similar decisions, creating a sort of "flattening of decisions" that causes the states themselves to lose ground from a competitive point of view. The algorithms are also transparent and partly accessible to third parties who, potentially, can discover and predict the strategy and future moves of software, taking advantage of them and creating discrepancies in markets and international ports. For all these reasons, several countries are backtracking and seem intent on returning to more traditional systems of government.

Beyond borders

Before going any further, it is useful to remember once again that nation states are a relatively recent invention and that, like any form of government in the history of mankind, they are strongly linked to the economy and society from which they derive. We need to turn to the past and the main anthropological treaties if we want to look more closely at the issue of states and their forms of government. Let's start from the studies of Robin Dunbar, who has shown that each individual is able to interact with up to 150 other individuals. The rule applies to all types of interaction, whether physical – that with people who live in our city and who we meet every day for work, business or pleasure – or generated online, through chat, programs and social networks. Although thanks to the web we believe we interact with many more people, the reality is that we manage real contact with a maximum number of 150. If it seems to you a small figure, consider that this ability to interact is an exclusive peculiarity of human beings who, compared to other animals, maintain more connections with their peers. The fact remains, however, that in the history of mankind we have evolved to create groups of individuals who far exceed this number. How is it possible, then, that we have gone from small communities of hunters and gatherers (essentially extended families) to real agricultural villages (about ten thousand years ago), to cities, fiefdoms, kingdoms and empires? The answer lies in the trick of the hierarchy: we have created a social system in which everyone, while continuing to have access to the "magic" number of 150 individuals, is able to interact with increasingly large and complex communities. The leader interacts in a group of 150 individuals, each of them interacting in turn with another 150 and so on. If there were no overlaps between individuals and groups, in a single step, we would have already reached a total interaction of 2,500 individuals. This system worked for several centuries, during which, as a result, the inhabitants of a kingdom or empire were not defined as citizens of a geographical area but as subjects of a ruler. Subsequently, some fundamental historical passages have changed the conditions: the Peace of Westphalia, in 1648, put an end to the Thirty Years' War and sanctioned the national sovereignty of the existing states, providing a foundation for modernity. Then, the fall of the Austro-Hungarian Empire in 1918 redesigned the borders of Europe, creating national states with geographical borders established on the basis of the linguistic and cultural communities of the inhabitants.[33] Within a few years, governments began to manage their countries more efficiently, granting voting rights to citizens who, in this way, had acquired a greater sense of belonging and participation to the administration of the Public Thing. In 2020, citizens identified with their state, rather than with who was governing them at that time.

The future, however, as we know, always brings change. In 2050, the idea of nation states defined by geographical boundaries is becoming obsolete. More and more communities, united not by citizenship but by the sharing of similar values and ideals, are taking root, claiming their autonomy. In 2050, some communities have rules which, by international convention, are added to those of the state to which its members belong, provided that they do not contradict the latter. Many of these communities reside on platforms such as Bitnation,[34] which, by exploiting blockchain technology (specifically Ethereum), allows its users to create a new country with its own constitution, laws, governance and services. While, in 2020, Bitnation only offered the Pangea service (a kind of decentralized market for legal services and little more), in 2050, instead, it manages education, medical care, personal services, social services, financial instruments and much more, and has its own agency for space exploration.

In addition to these terrestrial communities, there are also spaces, such as Asgardia,[35] which, with only two years of life in 2018, had almost 280,000 active citizens, a constitution and a parliament elected through regular elections.

HISTORY OF PANARCHY

The idea that it is possible to create states regardless of territorial boundaries (*panarchy*) was born in 1860, by a botanist named Paul Émile de Puydt. His theories went unnoticed for a long time, at least until the twenty-first century, when John Zube and Gian Piero de Bellis brought them back into fashion.
Since then, interest has grown exponentially, so much so as to involve a group of thinkers from Silicon Valley who, thanks to the use of new technologies, believe that it is possible to rethink the concept of nationality, completely detaching it from geographical boundaries and leaving it to the free choice of citizens who choose under which political regime to live, independently from the place in which they reside.[36]

Wars and technology

Drones capable of turning into formidable snipers, exoskeletons that allow soldiers to become superhumans, wars simulated by advanced artificial intelligence, cyber attacks and battles between robots, biological weapons and insects genetically modified to spread diseases: the war landscape of 2050 can certainly be scary.

Many weapons are autonomous, that is, they do everything by themselves. Think of drones, used as fierce and very precise snipers, and robots able to locate a target and fire without the need for a human command.

The use of autonomous weapons has understandably triggered major debates from the earliest projects. Many questions are asked. For example, when an autonomous weapon kills someone, who is it that "pulled the trigger"? Who is accountable: the robot, the person who commands the army, or the man or woman who designed and manufactured the weapon? What are the psychological consequences for a soldier who, sitting in front of a computer, decides the life and death of the opponents? Is it OK for a robot to be able to hurt a human being? Or should every machine be designed to defend human life at all times under all circumstances? And again: with biological weapons and those that use genetic editing, how strong is the risk that something escapes the control of human beings and that epidemics or uncontrollable mutations arise? These deep and almost infinite questions have always troubled human beings.

These are the same dilemmas that Ludovico Ariosto talked about when, in *Orlando Furioso*, he harshly condemned the creators of the arquebus, an invention that gave Orlando enormous and undeserved advantages against Cimosco, king of Friesland. Orlando, after beating the king, throws away the weapon and uses harsh words to argue that it is an instrument produced by the devil as a means of destroying the world, capable of making those who do not reflect the virtues of the true knight stronger. What would Orlando say if he saw soldiers in front of a computer miles away from the battlefield attack others and command drones and deadly weapons? And what would he have thought of the destructive power of the atomic bomb?

In 1950, one of the greatest theoretical physicists after Einstein was arrested by the agents of Scotland Yard for surrendering to the Soviet Union the secrets of the atomic bomb and the hydrogen bomb. His name was Klaus Fuchs and he was sentenced to a handful of years in prison for his treason. When questioned, he exposed another spy and set in motion a chain reaction process that led to the electrification of the Rosenberg couple, who were accused of espionage against the United States. In the 1990s, it was discovered that among those who had passed on essential information to the Soviet Union there was also the vainest of the physicists stationed in Los Alamos: Ted Hall. In an interview, Hall stated that he had not done so because of pro-Soviet tendencies but, on the contrary, for fear of leaving a weapon so destructive that it could upset the balance of mankind forever in the hands of a single entity (the United States). Similarly, the young Richard Feynman, another theoretical physicist with an exceptional mind, initially refused to work on the construction of the atomic bomb. In his books he says that he overcame his initial reluctance for fear that another opposing power might come to build the horde before the United States, thus threatening the lives of many of his fellow citizens.

These stories teach us three important things:

- Technological progress is inevitable. It's part of us and our evolution. There always seems to be a reason that makes it ethically right to invent a new technology and perfect it, there is always a positive

use, whether it is a new cure for cancer or the way to avoid a rare genetic disease or the realization of defensive weapons.
- For millennia, Homo sapiens have built objects and invented ways to increase their physical and intellectual abilities. For millennia these have been used to do both good and evil.
- There are inventions and technologies that can release enormous power and change the destiny of mankind. Trying to maintain a balance between the world powers, making these inventions available to all, on an equal footing, should be the priority of humanity.

Robotics, genomics and artificial intelligence could have the destructive power of an atomic bomb if used with intent and aggressive warfare. Elon Musk understood this well. After comparing artificial intelligence to the atomic bomb, in 2015 he was one of the founders of OpenAI, a non-profit organization whose objective is to provide everybody with the expensive tools necessary for the development of artificial intelligence, thus avoiding excessive polarization and concentration of power on specific subjects and countries.

Technological or otherwise, war is always war, and inevitably brings with it suffering, pain, destruction and loss of life. In 2050, unfortunately, this has not changed.

AGAINST AUTONOMOUS WEAPONS

In the first decades of the year 2000, there have been global movements against the use of artificial intelligence in the military field. In particular, the debate in the United States is very heated since there has been a wave of protests by employees of large technology companies such as Google and Amazon, who do not want the systems developed with their contribution to be made available for military purposes. Google, for example, decided not to renew the Maven project, linked to artificial intelligence algorithms used in military drones, and announced that it does not want to participate in the tender launched by the Pentagon for the creation of a cloud computing system. Jeff Bezos, founder of Amazon, is of a completely different opinion: despite employee protests, Bezos has claimed he will support the government in developing its own technology and stressed the fact that it is a tool and that the moral value of the actions carried out using it depends on the intentions of those who control it.

> Meanwhile, against the creation of autonomous weapons, one of the technological applications in the field of warfare, a global movement #bankillerrobots has already collected more than 26,000 signatures including that of Stephen Hawking, Noam Chomsky, Elon Musk, Steve Wozniak and many other prominent names among researchers, scientists, philosophers, entrepreneurs, citizens and activists. The petition can be found at http://autonomousweapons.org and calls for a ban on the development of tools that can kill without identifying a human being on whom responsibility lies.

Currency

A matter of trust

Like most human relationships, the monetary system is based on trust. Trust between people, who make an exchange behind the guarantee of the currency, and trust in institutions, who certify the validity and value of the currency in use in a given context. In the past, however, the problem of trust was less central, because the value of money was inherent in the very material with which it was made (for example, gold, silver, bronze). Things changed with the introduction of the banknote: a sheet of paper certifying the bearer's possession of a quantity of gold kept in the coffers of an empire or a kingdom. The first experiments with banknotes were made in China, in the ninth century, under the Yuan dynasty. Marco Polo gives us his testimony in the pages of his famous diary. The new method was not easily accepted by all, so much so that, in order to make its use obligatory, it was necessary to resort to a brutal law that threatened those who refused to accept a banknote as compensation for an exchange with the death penalty. On the banknotes was written a guarantee that they were valid for an unlimited period and would always be convertible into the gold value associated with them. The experiment, however, failed miserably: the regents had issued bank notes for a much higher value than the real gold stocks kept in the imperial coffers, thus betraying the promise of convertibility and the trust of the people, who, realizing the deception during the first period of famine, immediately abandoned this form of payment.

The banknotes reappeared in Europe 800 years later, in the seventeenth century, thanks to goldsmiths. At that time it was not easy to purchase gold directly or quickly, so goldsmiths, who already owned the metal, issued a receipt to trusted customers: a certificate of goldsmithery. All other merchants trusted the goldsmiths and became accustomed to using these certificates as a means of exchange: no one had any doubts about their convertibility. Again, trust played a key role but, unlike in China, the result was positive. From then on, this method of payment began to spread widely, until it was adopted directly by governments, which collaborated to issue banknotes on the basis of the gold kept in state coffers.

In 1971, the then President of the United States, Richard Nixon, took a decision that changed the history of capital forever, and freed the value of the banknotes from the amount of gold stored in the state coffers. The time was ripe, the trust mechanisms were in place and, above all, the choice had been considered and officially clarified to everyone: the experiment that had failed in China more than a thousand years earlier became a reality. At that point the currency began to be considered as a means in itself, increasingly free from paper or metal, so much so that the transition to digital tools has been fast: virtual transactions ordered with credit cards, ATMs, online transfers and apps on smartphones are now considered normal.

CASH

If you are particularly fond of cash, maybe you will change your mind, keeping in mind that:

- When the SARS broke out, to prevent contagion, payments by credit cards only were accepted on planes. Notes and coins, in fact, are one of the largest vehicles of dirt and disease.
- If you lose a banknote or a coin, as they are bearer securities it is not possible to recover them or track their movements in any way.
- Three out of every 10,000 banknotes in circulation in the United States are estimated to be counterfeit.
- Cash is expensive for the state because storing it requires a lot of space.

Cryptocurrencies

Now that we know how the monetary system has evolved, it will be easier to understand how, in 2050, cash has become just a memory. Free from the constraints of gold and physical means of payment, the citizens of 2050 have opted for the use of cryptocurrency: electronic coins. China, followed by some Arab countries, was the first country to decide to adopt a state system of cryptocurrency based on blockchain.

Initially, alongside the traditional currency, in 2050 the cryptocurrency system gradually replaced, throughout the world, traditional currencies, until it became the only recognized form of currency. The success of cryptocurrencies is based on the fact that they are secured by cryptocode strings and can be exchanged relatively confidentially (but not anonymously) and with the guarantee given by the blockchain system, which makes it impossible to multiply – and thus falsify – the coins in circulation. Everything takes place without the constraint of physicality and without the need for an intermediary (for example, a bank).

The blockchain is a database – shared and distributed – of transactions between several parties, designed to increase transparency, security and efficiency. Historically, organizations have always used central data files for the certification and evaluation of information. Advances in software, communications and cryptography have made it possible to build, instead, a decentralized system, in which information on transactions is propagated through the network, spreading among the various nodes that are part of the chain (*blockchain* can be translated literally as "chain of blocks, of nodes"). In its purest form (as when used for cryptocurrency), the blockchain is a kind of digital ledger of the transactions – recorded and verified – of a network of participants – that create a chain of actions visible to all.

This distributed control system keeps track of all changes of ownership and thus of all transactions that have taken place since the cryptocurrency code in question was created. It is as if today we were to report on each banknote all the passages of ownership to which it has been subject, making it spendable only by its last, legitimate, owner. Unlike the banknotes to which we are accustomed in the present, cryptocurrencies, therefore, are not bearer securities. In addition, once a payment is made with a cryptocurrency, it is no longer possible to cancel the transaction, which remains permanently recorded in the list of property passages.

The transfer of ownership takes place in a network, between the accounts of the two parties concerned that have the function of true virtual portfolios. In this operation there is no need for an intermediary, because the validation of the transaction is carried out through the other nodes of the network on which all the "historical" information has been distributed that allow a code to be verified or not. Figures 11 and 12 schematize the process: every time a transaction takes place, from A to B and from B to C, the information is recorded in multiple nodes or servers (computers that create a distracted database of information) that simultaneously become custodians of the information. When C has to receive the cryptocurrency from B, the service, choosing randomly and not against the unstable some of the nodes of the network, answers by certifying that B, at that moment, has the right of possession of the code in question and that the transaction can take place. The currency exchanged in this way will forever carry with it the history of the transfers of ownership, since the latter can only take place on the blockchain.

Figure 11   Exemplification of the relationships among subjects on a blockchain network

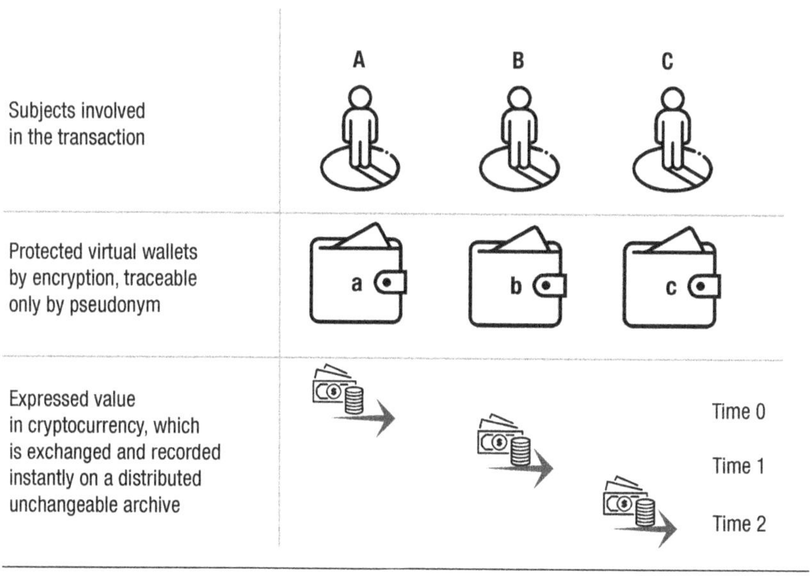

	A	B	C
Subjects involved in the transaction	👤	👤	👤
Protected virtual wallets by encryption, traceable only by pseudonym	a	b	c
Expressed value in cryptocurrency, which is exchanged and recorded instantly on a distributed unchangeable archive	💰→	💰→	💰→	Time 0 / Time 1 / Time 2

Figure 12 Certification of information without centralized intermediaries

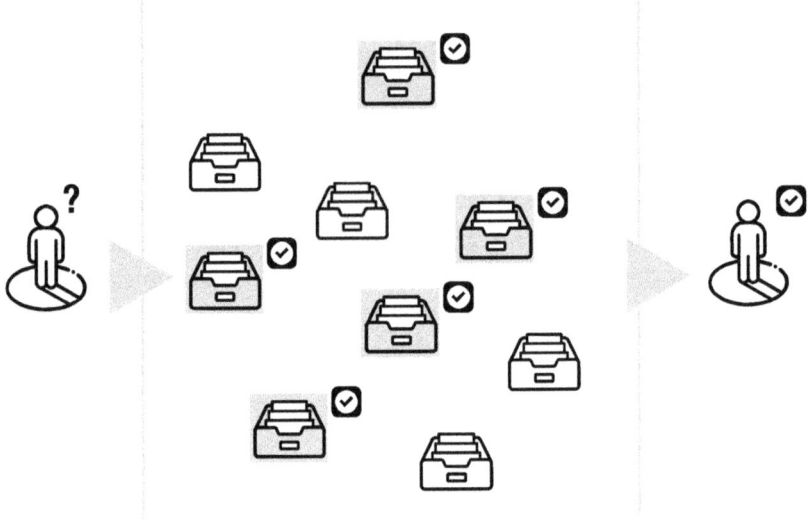

But who's in charge of issuing the new coins? Easy: it's the system itself. The coins, in fact, are generated automatically and distributed in the network following a geometric series that tends asynchronously to a predetermined limit. The nodes, therefore, can be both simple custodians of information and emitters of currency. In this way, the amount of currency in circulation is always controlled and known a priori by all.

Experiments

In 2050, cryptocurrencies are in turmoil and are becoming the vehicle for local experiments that could greatly change the principles underlying economies.

Beyond state cryptocurrencies, there is a whole series of new virtual currencies that represent a real way of life: impactcoins, which are linked to the positive impact generated by the individual; environmentcoins, which reward the protection of the environment; educoins, which measure the level of education, and many other tools linked to complex formulas of citizens' ratings, usually accepted as means of payment by shops, companies, individuals and governments.

THE ADVANTAGES OF THE BLOCKCHAIN

What are the real advantages of the blockchain? Why did it change so much in 2050? Let's look at the main ones:

- *Security*: blockchain relies on encryption to validate transactions, verifying the identities of the parties involved.
- *Transparency*: by its nature, blockchain is a database distributed, managed and synchronized among multiple nodes. According to its design, multiple parties can access the same data (in some cases locally within their organizations).
- *Efficiency*: blockchain eliminates the possibility of conflicting data between multiple databases, avoiding the need for manual reconciliations.

In 2020 the blockchain was just over ten years old and to realize the applications of 2050 it was necessary to overcome many critical issues such as the scalability of the system, the cryptographic security put at test by the advent of quantum computers and the lack of a unified governance on the network. However, once the scepticism and criticism had been overcome, this technology flourished.

Because of all the advantages listed, many contracts and transactions in 2050 are based on the blockchain mechanism: public registers (registries, degrees, curriculum vitae), tax collection systems, contracts between individuals and between companies, marriages (which automatically and immediately regulate the possibility of a divorce), wills, registers of ratings and reliability, titles of ownership of companies, houses, objects of all kinds, and documents for sharing and use of energy and water.

If you still have doubts about the functioning and the real advantages of such a system, we can try to do a little experiment and imagine two kindergarten children deciding to conclude a deal. Fabio is in his final year and his locker is marked with a unicorn sticker, which Laura, a younger kid, desires ardently. All the other children recognize that that locker is Fabio's. One day the two decide to make a deal: when Fabio finishes kindergarten in June, he will give Laura the locker. In return, until June, Laura will offer Fabio her daily snack. But Laura, who is not naive, does not want to give up her snack without having guarantees: How can she, next year, enforce her agreement with Fabio against other children? The two (and all other children) can't write and are too young to sign a contract. One solution could be to ask the teacher to act as an intermediary and certify that the locker will be Laura's next year. If the teacher agrees, you may still need to give her something in return for the mediation service.

Please note that if the teacher herself is influenced or if the information and certification are no longer accessible, someone may want to use that locker without knowing that it is owned by Laura. Fabio and Laura finally decide to proceed as follows, using the means available to them in class:

- Make a beautiful drawing, in which Fabio is portrayed handing over the ownership of the locker to Laura.
- Copy the drawing fifty times and enclose these in envelopes, each marked with the symbol of a different playing card.
- When someone wants to know the ownership of the unicorn locker, or simply prove that it is Laura's, they just have to ask for access to one of the envelopes. To make sure there are no tricks, he or she will draw ten playing cards and open the envelopes bearing the symbols of the cards drawn. Inside each envelope, will be a copy of the original drawing, proving Laura's right to the locker.

With this procedure it is not possible to cheat, because the formation is distributed in fifty different envelopes, kept in different places, and the choice of which to open is random. The system is transparent because, potentially, anyone can ask to verify the information without necessarily having to go to a central database (in our case the teacher): it is also reserved because it does not require the owner (Laura) to make the information public by placing her photo on the locker.

1 SNAPSHOT OF 2050

ROBOCHAIN

The blockchain is not a technology that is entirely the preserve of humans. In fact, in 2050 there are many more robots, objects and algorithms connected to blockchain than humans. Objects such as washing machines, solar panels and household batteries, self-driving cars and service robots use the blockchain continuously to communicate with each other and to carry out various types of transactions.

For example, the home refrigerator might discover that some food is missing and order it from an online service, just as the washing machine might buy detergent, or the home solar panel might give away part of the excess energy accumulated to the nearby battery. The advantage of this system is that it also allows transactions for very small values without exorbitant costs or complications due to long waiting times (as would happen using bank transfers of 2020).

2050
TODAY

TIMER LTD LAUNCHES A NEW PRODUCT: FIXED-TERM TEN-YEAR MARRIAGES

After the success of weddings with a fixed-term duration of twenty-five years, Timer Ltd launches a new light version on the market. Fixed-term marriages, in fact, are more fashionable among those who, thanks to genetic treatments with stem cells, believe they will have a life expectancy of more than 120 years.

The new product, on the other hand, is aimed at a segment of the population with a shorter life expectancy, in search of a solution more suited to their needs. The service, based on blockchain, provides a fixed-term marriage that ceases to exist after ten years. The company takes care of all the details of the divorce automatically.

Society, work and education

Progress, utopias and dystopias

Human beings have always loved to tell stories of extraordinary places and eras, in the past and in the future, and imagine fantastic societies that are useful as models for the real world. The ancient Greeks, for example, regretted the golden age that had degenerated because of moral corruption, caused by luxury, jewellery, weapons, hierarchies and rules, and then ended in the bloodshed of the Trojan War. Lucretius, in *De Rerum Natura*, identifies the source of this degeneration in progress as fed by human inventions. More luxury would require more technological and social tools to produce, defend and control, thus creating more complexity and more conflict.

If Lucretius' vision of progress has not evolved enough to be considered without adequate contextualization (for example, the Latin poet did not foresee the possibility of future changes), it serves in any case as a testimony to the fact that technology, inventions, past and future, have been intertwined for thousands of years in the stories on which the cultures of humanity are based. Stories written, recounted and imagined in an attempt to identify truly attainable paths of well-being and happiness.

With the same intent, Plato told us about Atlantis: a model of society that embodied his political ideals. And he did so in such detail and in such a convincing way that many people believed in the existence of this legendary island.

In 1516 it was the turn of Thomas More, who, on this occasion, came to terms with *utopia*. Using the ploy of showing a perfect and positive imaginary alternative, he succeeded in his real goal: to harshly criticize the society in which he lived. To do so he described this place, Utopia, as a sort of "island that does not exist", a "non-place" where there is no private property and everyone does a job in line with their personal inclinations and has sufficient free time to devote to culture. An ideal world where education, creativity and harmony reign over society. The term utopia has since spread rapidly, embodying the concept of an ideal society and, for this reason, impossible to achieve.

The opposite of a utopia is a *dystopia*: a place where everything is distorted, a society in which the tools that could make great things possible (at least according to the hopes of the good) have become the cause of unimaginable limitations of freedom. We are bringing this up this because 2050 is a destination that has been the subject of much speculation. There are reports of travellers who have visited a utopian 2050 and others of travellers who have visited a totally dystopian one. Who's right? Who says that the future, thanks to technology, is a happy society, where human beings no longer work, replaced by robots, and can therefore dedicate their free time to art, culture and entertainment? Or who, fearing automation and the advent of machines, affirms it will seriously endanger humanity itself?

In 1945, Karl Popper, in his book *The Open Society and its Enemies*, wrote that utopian visions presuppose the existence of a closed system, a society that ends up transforming itself into a violent attack towards reality and people in an attempt to delimit them within boundaries that do not reflect the facts and, therefore, we add, becomes a kind of dystopia that deprives people of freedom, since it ends up imposing an unrealistic model.[37]

In general, the advice is to be wary of those who predict a future with too extreme characteristics, whether positive or not. However, you can and must listen to them and use their stories to understand which models are possible and which ones should be avoided: only by knowing both perspectives can you travel to a 2050 that really reflects your expectations.

If, on the other hand, you stop dreaming, you may find yourself in a stalemate situation with no prospects.

Changes

Automation, new energy sources, decentralization: in the future, these trends influence society and the working environment in a very profound way. Much of the work we were used to in 2020, in fact, in 2050 can be carried out indifferently by both humans and robots, with a consequent increase in pace and efficiency in many areas, including competition and energy needs.

NEW ENERGY SOURCES

Among the new sources used in 2050 to meet the growing demand for energy we can include:

- nuclear fission: an expensive and non-renewable solution
- hydroelectric, solar and wind energy: now much more efficient in conserving the energy produced thanks to new graphene batteries
- solar energy produced by structures located in space: a visionary and very expensive project even in 2050, a project still in its infancy, to which, however, a lot of attention is being paid because it has great potential.

In this climate of great novelty, the only certainty is that change reigns supreme and that things happen very quickly. In 2050 as never before, you need to be flexible and have a spirit of adaptation.

THE SUPERMAN DILEMMA

Transversal impacts between sectors, changes and flexibility: Is it really necessary to reinvent oneself and change one's habits so as not to be left behind? Let's give an example.
Let's imagine that we are Superman in 2050: compared to 1990 the world has changed. The spread of mobile phones first, and then of wearable and implantable devices, has deprived us of two fundamental things: a safe place to change in case of emergencies and the privacy necessary to keep our identity secret. It's an unexpected impact, caused by technology that, not being directly related to our work, we didn't think would damage us. Yet, today, that technology prevents us from doing our job, posing a dilemma: Stop saving defenseless citizens or try to understand how to use the new technology to work differently?
Let's think about it: we could, for example, download a car-sharing application on our device that allows us not only to change in a car, but also, if we choose a self-driving vehicle, to reach the desired place while we do it. All while preserving our privacy.

In this context, modern energy sources – capable of fuelling this industrial revolution that is making every person, product or service smart, connected and decentralized – are essential.

An example of a sector subject to great change is that of intercontinental transport: on the one hand, the greater specialization and concentration of agricultural production in certain geographical and graphic areas increases the demand for intercontinental transport, opening up new opportunities for those who wish to invest in this area; on the other hand, 3D printing, which has become increasingly efficient and fast, allows the decentralization of the production of objects made with any material and eliminates the need to transport them from one part of the world to another. New summer trade routes opened in the Arctic because of the seasonal melting of sea ice and faster means of transport have also made it easier to move and changed the balance that was stable for centuries (we will see better when talking about the climate).

NEW TRADE ROUTES

After the aforementioned race for artificial intelligence, the race for trade routes is one of the forces shaping the future and 2050. This battle has been going on for a long time. In 2018 we witnessed the first Arctic voyage of an icebreaker cargo ship that opened up new routes by exploiting the thinning of ice in the summer months. It was Maersk Line, the world's largest maritime transport company, that experimented with an ancient route in northern Russia, in search of an alternative to the Suez Canal. Still expensive in 2020 despite the reduced time, in 2050 this and other routes tested in the north-east or north-west allow one to save up to twelve days compared to the Suez route. In 2050, China is even testing a transpolar route: from the Strait of Bering directly to Iceland via a straight route through the North Pole.

Jobs

In 2050 it is normal not only to change jobs often, but also to have several jobs and sources of income at the same time, with mechanisms such as sharing flats or the granting of data on one's habits and DNA (data which in some cases are paid for generously).

NEW SECTORS AND NEW JOBS

In the world of work, some of the most bustling sectors are:

- *Ecology*: those who are able to rehabilitate polluted environments and ecosystems are key.
- *Neurotechnologies and neurosciences*: those capable of programming and maintaining cyborgs are sought after.
- *Private space exploration*: the sector employs many scientists and engineers.
- *Entertainment and gamification*: the ability to create new forms of immersive experiences is highly desired.
- *Security*: the risk of hacking now affects everything and everyone and quantum computing experts are in high demand.
- *Ethics*: artificial intelligence, robotics, biotechnology and genomics pose profound ethical dilemmas for the inhabitants of 2050 and the profession of philosopher is increasingly in demand.
- *Certification and harmonization of algorithms*: information technicians are needed to make algorithms comparable between one country to another (e.g. autonomous driving algorithms which must be adapted to different road codes).
- *Data science*: the interpretation of data collected and processed by algorithms is a very valuable role.
- *Psychology*: in particular, therapists specialized in the use of virtual reality and augmented reality are required, as well as consultants for the design of these tools, who work closely with artificial intelligence.
- *The architecture of complex systems*: requires those capable of designing efficient interactions between robots, algorithms, humans and institutions.
- *The management of new resources*: almost all companies are introducing a robotic resources manager into their organization, who works alongside the "classic" human resources manager for better management of all types of employees.
- *Robot design*.
- *DNA design*.

Many brokerage jobs have changed dramatically since 2020, many even no longer exist because they have not been able to adapt. More and more products are being replaced by services based on decentralized platforms,[38] transfers of ownership (and the related intermediation) are less required and, when necessary, thanks to the blockchain can be finalized without the need to turn to a notary, a bank or an institution. Many of the services carried out in the past by human beings, in 2050 are carried out by robots and algorithms, with the consequent need to relocate workers who remain unemployed. Algorithms and machines, in fact, not only cost less than humans, but are also tireless, work without the need to take breaks (seven days a week and twenty-four hours a day) and in some cases are much more efficient. In 2050, artificial intelligence machines became excellent translators, therapists, bestseller writers, financial experts, logistical operators, trainers, doctors, surgeons and postmen. There is no field of work that does not make extensive use of these tools. But this does not mean that the future of humans is a future without work: simply, the role of humans has changed, as has the approach to work.

New jobs: Robot designer

Trust is one of the pillars on which human interactions are based. A good dose of confidence is formed, depending on the qualities of our brain, based on the appearance of others, his or her way of moving, tone of voice, facial expressions and odours. This process is the result of centuries of evolution of our species and is an integral part of us. What happens if, in the world we know, in our society, we find ourselves interacting every day with robotic creatures who have a completely new way of expressing themselves and moving? How important is their appearance and the impression they give us when they interact with us or provide us with a service? This not only matters a great deal, but is the key that justifies the spread of one model of robot over another.

Robot designers, therefore, are experts in psychology, design and emotion, who recreate social intelligence in machines and learn how to make them interact with human beings.

2050 TODAY

12-YEAR-OLD HIRED BY AI ALGORITHM: SELECTED FROM THOUSANDS OF CANDIDATES

The Recruiter algorithm was doing its usual routine work when, last Tuesday, he finally selected the ideal candidate for an open position for a well-known Indian pharmaceutical company. After analyzing the social profiles, the interactions with other users, the data available online and the interview given via chat, Recruiter felt that Mario J. Francis was just the right person. Privacy filters did not allow age to be used as a rating parameter and the system did not realize that it had illegally hired a minor.
Now Mario claims his right to accept the job, but the current regulations do not allow this.

Technological unemployment and social nets

For every job lost due to machines, the First Industrial Revolution was able to create a new one, at the same time improving the living conditions of workers. Why then should things have gone differently with the advent of artificial intelligence? The answer lies in the convergence of this new technology with the medical-scientific revolution linked to discoveries on DNA, stem cells and the brain. It is no longer a question of replacing manual skills or human strength, but of our ability to make decisions. In 2050 we are faced with machines that are able to imitate the functioning of our intuition, replicating its activities. For this reason, all jobs known today are influenced by new technologies: either because a machine (or a network of machines) is able to do that job better than a human being, or because a rapid and profound change in the way it is done is required. In both cases, social nets are needed for the workers. The various experiments under way in 2050 follow, in particular, three strands:

- *State training*. Some countries have decided to focus on the education and to train, with the support of institutions, schools and universities, workers to be able to perform the tasks required by the new jobs. This type of training is often provided en masse and is fully supported, in terms of costs, by the state, as an investment to

employ citizens and to restart the economy where there are companies in crisis due to a lack of qualified personnel. Often workers take advantage of this training opportunity several times during their career, since the usefulness of certain tasks for the market has only lasted, on average, ten years.
- *Taxes on robots.* Proposed for the first time by Bill Gates in the first decades of the century, this solution provides for the introduction of a tax on the work of robots, as if they were human beings. This tax has been used as a tool to slow down the change that otherwise would have happened too quickly to allow society to adapt. Thanks to this, by 2050 the automation of many jobs was more gradual and the funds raised via this route were used to retrain former human workers.
- *Universal basic income.* In some countries, universal basic income has been provided for a long time: a median income supplied by the state to all citizens, regardless of any other sources of income they may have. The basic idea is not to make any difference in order not to create disincentivising mechanisms: if I receive a cheque that is sufficient for me to reach a minimum level of well-being only if I do not work, I may not be encouraged to look for a job. In some cases this system has worked, creating a climate of greater security and freedom for the citizens involved, who are more inclined to follow their passions, giving rise to entrepreneurial projects, without the thought of income having to be dominant. In other situations, however, citizenship income has proved to be a double-edged sword and has helped to increase laziness and torpor. Creativity, one of the most sought-after skills in the world or work, is often damaged by a universal basic income. Creativity, in fact, develops and flourishes in problematic or difficult situations, contexts in which there are limits to be overcome or shortages. If I have everything I need to recreate a traditional irrigation system to supply water to my plants, I will find it difficult to find a more efficient, less expensive solution; if I find myself in a situation of scarcity of resources, or time, I will try to find an alternative creative solution that allows me to solve the problem with what I have available. For example, crucial innovations in the field of space exploration came from the assumption that we would have to survive in an environment where there is nothing we need, so we must necessarily become efficient.

According to this logic, the profitability of universal basic income, guaranteeing an "easy" solution for all, has flattened the level of creativity in many situations. Moreover, the mechanism is often a source of inflation: the prices of all products and services, in fact, increase in proportion to the cheque to which the citizens are entitled, returning the economy to its initial position.

A THOUSAND-YEAR-OLD DREAM

Already in the tenth century bc we have evidence, in China, of the construction of a robot with human features. It is said that this robot, made by Yan Shin, a mechanical engineer, was able to dance and sing, inspiring the admiration of King Mu. No matter if it's a legend, this story is one of the earliest examples of human engineering; humans have always dreamed of building creatures to replace them in manual labour.
For the first physical proof, we must, however, wait until the third century bc. This time we are in Byzantium and we are in front of the Automatic Servant of Philon: a machine with human features, able to pour the wine at the request of the guests (placing the cup on the left hand of the statue, the mechanism is activated and pours the precious liquid from a jug held in his right hand).
The art of building robots, therefore, is not a modern technique, but a discipline born more than three thousand years ago that over the centuries has been pursued for the most disparate purposes: war, ornament, entertainment and religion.

ROBOTS OF THE WORLD, UNITE!

In 2020, the discussion on the effects of automation on the workplace is central. In an article published in the Washington Post,[39] Feng Xiang, an expert professor of law, introduced the theme of unemployment resulting from the growing application of artificial intelligence:
"The most important challenge facing socio-economic systems today is the arrival of artificial intelligence. If artificial intelligence remains under the control of market forces, it will inexorably lead to a super-rich oligopoly of billionaire data holders who collect the wealth created by robots that move human labour, leaving behind massive unemployment."

But this, according to his vision, would not be the only possible evolution and the answer could be in the hands of the Chinese socialist economy. In fact, "If artificial intelligence rationally assigns resources to big data analysis, and if robust feedback loops can supplant the imperfections of the 'invisible hand' by fairly sharing the vast wealth it creates, a planned economy that actually works could finally be achievable. Artificial intelligence would therefore be the ideal tool to put an end to capitalism."

Feng Xiang sees the nationalization of artificial intelligence and the most innovative technological solutions as the only way to avoid mass technological dislocation. The article closes provocatively as follows:

"If properly regulated in this way, we should celebrate, not fear, the advent of artificial intelligence. If it is brought under social control, it will make workers free to devote their time to the enrichment of those at the top. The communism of the future should adopt a new slogan: 'Robots of the world, unite!'"

Marx and machines

Communism and automation are linked in a very intimate way: Marx dedicated many pages to this theme and it might be useful to read them again to deepen our own understanding.

Capitalism has, according to Marx, some macro-trends, one of which is automation. Marx observes that, in order to increase profits, the capitalist is in a sense forced to increase productivity and can do so by increasing total working hours, or by investing their earnings in innovation in the production process. This means investing in technology and automation to make the process more efficient and lower personnel costs. A wave mechanism is thus created whereby resources (labour) are freed up to become part of what Marx calls the "reserve industrial army" and then reabsorbed in a successful phase of increasing production, until a new phase is grafted on. The sum, however, is not zero and the result is that this exercise increases over time. In the words of Stefano Petrucciani, "the second trend will certainly prevail, that is to say, the trend towards the growing creation of surplus labour, but it will not be affirmed in a linear manner, but will go through a cyclical process of contraction and expansion of the surplus labour force itself".[40] This is why the trend towards automation leads to the so-called "technological unemployment" so much discussed in the contemporary world.

However, Marx does not stop there and, among other things, draws the conclusion that a world that has become a slave to the law of capitalist accumulation can only lead to a concentration of power in the hands of a few major players. An undeniable trend, to say the least. But beware: as Petrucciani reminds us, if we read *The Capital*, we will be called to order. The equation wouldn't be "more machines = more unemployment" but "capitalist system = unemployment and alienation". The interesting point is that, according to Marx, we have to look at the economic system and not at automation itself in order to find the real cause of the problem, as also mentioned by James Mill, John Stuart Mill, John McCulloch, Robert Torrens and Nassau Senior.[41] We should start from a careful observation of society rather than from technology to understand the problem and try to trace it back to its main nucleus. What few have yet understood, however, is that to analyse the problem of technological unemployment, we should begin to look at man and not at the machine. Because it is only by trying to understand our nature that we can try to outline the future evolutions of work, keeping our fundamental values firmly in place.

The vision of the future that we want to set ourselves as an achievable goal is important in this sense. According to Marx, in the future we will find ourselves living in a world where, to quote Petrucciani once again, "misery and antagonism cease and 'the free development of individuality' and 'the reduction of necessary work to a minimum for society, which then corresponds to the artistic, scientific, etc. form and development of individuals thanks to free time and the means created for all of them' take over".

We cannot fail to note that these words could have been uttered in 2020 in Silicon Valley by one of the many supporters of the universal basic income concept. Those who follow this position argue in fact that we will live in a world of abundance in the future and that we will devote ourselves to art, knowledge and culture, free at last from work once and for all.

But are we sure that's the only option? How many civilizations of the past had social classes perfectly capable of dedicating themselves to personal growth in their free time and yet did not create art, culture and innovations? What type of human nature would prevail in such a situation? Only by taking into account whether industriousness is a fundamental part of our nature can we really understand whether we can imagine a society free from work and fatigue. We must therefore approach the problem from the right perspective.

Let's start from human nature, from society and from the dreams on the basis of which society has developed to be what it is today, and let's try to imagine new forms of social interaction, new ways of doing business and conceiving work as expressions of our most intimate personalities.

Education and skills

There is only one theme on which the inhabitants of 2050 agree: education is – and must be – a central element in the life of all.

The changes that have affected the world of work have necessitated an adaptation of the educational systems, no longer conceived as a temporary phase, in preparation for a specific job, but a constant factor over time: training is continuous for all. In a situation of enormous uncertainty, characterized by changes and great speed, the only solution is to focus on skills and traits that are as transversal as possible and capable of being useful in various situations: creativity, flexibility, resilience, a critical spirit, the ability to work in groups, empathy and, above all, the ability to make decisions in increasingly complex contexts. For the students and workers of 2050 it is no longer a question of choosing a course of study based on the work they want to do for the rest of their adult lives, but of studying in depth what fascinates and stimulates their curiosity and creativity.

Education has, therefore, become a freer activity or, as Noam Chomsky would say,[42] freely participatory. Chomsky believes that educational practice should be designed to encourage creativity, exploration, independence, cooperation (i.e., he points out, the opposite of what has happened at the time of his writing, in 2017). His vision is in line with that of Alexander von Humboldt, a German naturalist, explorer and botanist who lived in the nineteenth century and who argued that education should be conceived as a taut thread along which students proceed in their own way, exercising and improving their creative abilities and imagination, and experiencing the joys of discovery. Both will be happy to see that what they dreamed of is the new paradigm of education in 2050. And that, thanks to this approach, the inhabitants of the future are able to reinvent themselves continuously.

CHILD'S PLAY

If in 2050 you decide to attend a course, you will certainly not fail nor will you take top marks: judgements no longer exist. On the contrary, you will be assessed on the basis of your knowledge, experience and skills. You will receive a sort of score similar to that of incentive systems such as Trip Advisor or those of video games, and the feedback exchanges between you and your teachers will be continuous, thanks to open and constant communication.

Unleash your superpower: The power of differences

Creativity, ethics, critical spirit, collaborative skills, empathy, flexibility, resilience and relational skills are certainly a good starting point. But human beings are characterized by great diversity, and there can be no one-size-fits-all method for success.

According to Adam Smith (1723–1790), social philosopher and economist, considered one of the fathers of capitalism, offering citizens the opportunity to exercise their intellect and to cultivate human development in its greatest diversity is the secret to a balanced society. In 2050, we are still a long way from a balance of this kind, but great strides have certainly been made. Never before has the theme of diversity at work been considered a strength, nor have individuals been able to express and enhance their talents and characteristics with as much freedom as in 2050.

The human factor

What makes a football game more exciting than a robot fight? Why do we appreciate a personalized service more than a fully automated service? What are the factors that most affect us when we watch a film or read a book? These questions dig deep, leading us to ask ourselves who we are and how we interact with each other, and can be summarized in a single fundamental question: What makes us human beings?

Abilities such as making decisions, collaborating, communicating, feeling sympathy and empathy, creating and planning for the future are typical characteristics of our species, qualities that distinguish and differentiate us from other creatures that inhabit our planet in 2050, such as cyborgs and robots. The human factor has taken on a new weight, a broader meaning that makes it extremely valuable: it has become the key to living in harmony in society and with technology. Towards the latter, in particular, a holistic and multidisciplinary approach has been developed that combines typical humanistic skills with technical skills, and has led to the creation of new professional figures such as genetic philosophers, expert linguists who program artificial intelligence and psychologists who devote themselves to robotics.

WHAT IS HUMAN?

What does the concept of "human" encompass in our culture? Is this a biological factor or a behavioural issue? In books, in films and in legends, a human is any creature who decides to act according to the values which we ourselves reflect, fighting the inhuman. We identify with and trust robots with artificial intelligence who decide to behave according to our canons; monsters who, despite their appearance, embody empathy and justice towards our species, and so on. In this sense, being human is not a genetic factor but a cultural one.
Leaving for the journey towards 2050, it is really crucial to establish what level of humanity we want to attribute to the many new creatures that populate our planet and who could, in the future, embody our values so as to be considered, accepting this definition, human like us.

Better together

The ability to collaborate is very important in 2050 and does not only concern humans, but also cyborgs and robots. It is a widely held opinion – proven by facts – that the greatest efficiency is achieved through collaboration between the different forms of existing intelligence and not by replacing humans with robots or vice versa. Many sports and mind-training quizzes aim to develop this new form of collaboration between man and machine and to encourage it as much as possible, to overcome diversity and create a peaceful climate of inclusion that also includes these new creatures.

Tools

Tools such as augmented reality and virtual reality are widely used at work and in education. The latter, in particular, allows you to train in a wide range of environments and situations, to hold meetings or lessons at a distance, and to learn skills such as creativity and empathy in an immersive and innovative way.

Love, reproduction and relationships

Paulo Coelho wrote: "The most important encounters are already combined by souls before the bodies can see each other."[43] If we replace the word "souls" with algorithms, we can get an idea of how relationships work in 2050.

Technological innovations have revolutionized the sexual habits and relationships of people of the future, creating new ways of connecting, reproducing and sharing intimacy. In order to understand the way in which relationships are managed, a summary of the most widespread reproduction techniques is necessary.

In 2050, reproduction and sexual intercourse are two aspects of human life that can be completely separated, with consequences for society and the management of interpersonal relationships.

"Designed" children and the outsourcing of reproduction

Genetic research, DNA discoveries and the use of stem cells have given rise – it must be said – to a new reproductive medicine that, on the one hand, allows new human beings to be born in a much safer way and without any risk for either mother or child, and, on the other hand, allows the same parents to choose before birth the preferred characteristics of their children, following a design process. Some people take advantage of the new functions provided by genetic advances to bring healthier children into the world, immediately treating any lethal malformations, or to "design" their children at will. In these cases, relatives no longer compete to see from whom the newborn has inherited the colour of the eyes, hair or other physical characteristics, because these distinctive features were decided in the laboratory well before birth.

Usually couples have only one child, as a result, households are smaller than in the past and invest more in having and raising a healthy and successful child. In the richest parts of the world, it is even possible to have a child without any physical involvement. Everything takes place in the laboratory: from conception to artificial gestation in the uterus to the most painful phase, the birth, which no longer exists in this process. The typical risks of this delicate moment are therefore very small and controlled.

SAME-SEX PARENTS

An experiment conducted in China has succeeded in creating laboratory mice that are the biological offspring of two female mice.[44] The baby mice are as healthy as those born, during the same study, from two male mice. The study wants to explore an unresolved question: Why do mammals need the genetic contribution of both the father and the mother while other animals such as sharks can reproduce without the material of the father? We know that the concept of imprinting plays an important role: each gene that is expressed in our DNA carries with it a kind of label that indicates whether it comes from the female or the male, and only the right mix of genes from the mother and father can create a healthy child. In the case of the Chinese study, scientists used genetic manipulation via the technique known as CRISPR-CAS9 to remove maternal imprinting from three crucial regions of DNA, making the genetic material more "masculine" in terms of imprinting pattern. The newborns, twenty-nine mice, led healthy lives into adulthood and also had healthy children.

The future parents, supported by artificial intelligence tools – which calculate in real time the best combination of their DNA – simply choose an embryo from those available and pick the related genes they prefer. At this point, mistakes can be corrected by inserting genes that are not part of the child's original genetic heritage. All traits can be personalized: the colour of the eyes, the hair, the size of the hands and feet, without forgetting the sex, the height and the colour of the skin. The variants obtained in this way are endless and are able not only to prevent any malformations or genetic diseases, but also to combine genes from more than two different people. In this context, therefore, everyone can have a child, regardless of the number of people involved, gender and age. There is even the possibility of producing semen from women and eggs from men in laboratories, thus allowing same-sex couples to have a child of whom the biological parents are both parties (provided that this is still considered an important factor given the way in which, in these parts of the world, the concept of reproduction is regarded).

THREE PARENTS

If you have been (or are) at least a little rebellious as a teenager, the idea of having more than two parents can certainly frighten you. Don't be afraid, however, when you discover that it is possible to have three parents: it is not a matter of growing up with an extra father or mother, but only of possessing DNA resulting from the crossing of genes from three (or more) different people.
The first experiments using this technique date back to 2016 and were developed to prevent the transmission of serious genetic diseases to children. During fertilization, an egg cell provides the genetic patrimony to the zygote; this part of the genetic patrimony – which does not influence a child's traits or the physical appearance – could carry with it some diseases such as deafness, blindness, diabetes and other disorders, including life-threatening ones. The technique then combines the genetic inheritance of the mother with that of a second woman (who in this way becomes a mother of 0.1% of the child), correcting the errors that cause possible diseases contained in the genetic heritage of the original egg. At this moment, this technique is only legal in Great Britain and a few other countries, as it is not clear whether long-term consequences can be expected.

In the image and likeness

More and more companies in the field of reproduction are allowing people to indulge themselves to the limits of their imagination. They allow potential parents to create children that are a real clone of one of the parents, starting from the simple nucleus of a cell and from any egg fertilized in vitro (deprived of its main nucleus). Others, on the other hand, promise, in a rather macabre message, to resurrect the dead, creating in the laboratory children who are the perfect clones of those who have already died. Finally, there are companies that have hundreds of models of "perfect" children in their catalogues: on a genetic level, such children have no part of the DNA of their parents and can be chosen from a list updated weekly. In most countries these techniques are not legal, but globally they are creating – as you might imagine – fierce ethical discussion.

Contraception

In the field of contraception, every woman has, if she wants, total control: natural pills and small microchips inserted under the skin reduce the probability of pregnancy to zero and allow almost total control over births.

Ethical dilemmas and social impacts

DNA has always been a subject that poses great ethical dilemmas. But when we think about it, it's normal: it's the code of our biological life, the recipe that makes us who we are and adapts to change, as we live our lives, storing information about ourselves and passing it on to our heirs.

In 2020, we have some tools to understand DNA, to read it, analyse it and to modify it. However, we have not yet reached a common agreement on what is or is not permissible in this area. Due to the different histories and cultures of the populations of the planet and the different religious imprints that characterize these, opinion varies greatly from country to country. But this is what commonly happens when it comes to innovations that touch so intimate and essential aspects of human life.

As in 2020, in 2050, too, there are people who have good reasons for supporting research in the field of reproduction, either due to a desire to have healthy children, or to a hope of curing those with life-threatening/limiting illnesses. They collect funds, invest and the research advances. Innovations and discoveries become routine over time, and someone thinks of starting to use them preventively to experience something new, out of love for science or out of curiosity or simply out of the desire to challenge the boundaries. Whatever the reason, until a shared set of cultural mores is established, the dilemma is destined to remain unresolved. So the scientists and researchers who continue to hope and those who continue, undaunted, to judge and prohibit the separation remain at loggerheads. The truth is that it is still too early to really understand the impacts that DNA changes can have in the long term on our species, and those who oppose them have the fundamental role of ensuring everyone is necessarily cautious.

This, however, is not the only problem that arises in the face of DNA-related discoveries. As we have already pointed out in relation to the population of 2050, there are innovations and technologies that cause great social divisions. This has happened for centuries with writing, electricity, household appliances and means of transport, and still happens today with medicine, genomics, access to the Internet and quality education. We could draw up endless lists of technologies that, accessible only to a few people, end up creating great inequalities.

In 2050, these disparities risk causing a particularly serious situation and creating different species of human beings: on the one hand, the rich, with enhanced cognitive abilities, healthy genetic characteristics that are perfect for adapting to the environment and being successful, and with a life expectancy of between 100 to 250 years; on the other hand, the poor, who, unable to afford capacity-building tools, are condemned to receive lower incomes, attend lower-level schools, be denied access to medical care and forms of genetic editing and have a life expectancy of only 80–90 years.

This is an enormous problem, which has always accompanied human beings and which has been accentuated in recent centuries, since the concepts of the individual and of human rights have developed to the point of becoming central to society.

New solutions are therefore needed to give everyone the same possibilities, regardless of the path chosen by each person to achieve happiness.

Deceiving nature

When the pill was introduced as a method of contraception in the 1960s, a real cultural revolution was triggered: this was a change that gave women greater freedom and progressively led them to play a very different role in relationships, at work and in society in general. In 2050, if possible, the change is even more profound. The separation between sexual intercourse and reproduction is completely changing the rules of the game. Until now, humans have evolved according to certain rules of courtship and mating. Complex rules that take into account DNA, environment and culture. In this context, physical appearance has a certain importance, as does social status and other factors that may influence an individual's chances of reproducing and continuing to live on in their heirs.

The ploy of nature to push us to reproduction is sexual pleasure. Even if we don't realize it, sexual pleasure is the means by which, unconsciously, we are seduced into achieving the real objective of nature: reproduction. If, with contraceptives, we put a stop to this and took a first step towards the possibility of obtaining pleasure without reproducing, in 2050 this millennial-old process has definitively been shattered: human beings can reproduce without sexual acts, they can mate without reproducing and, above all, they can do so with robots (see the subsection "Robots in love"). Everyone, therefore, can achieve sexual pleasure without striving to woo and bond with another human being.

What does it mean to be human in this context? How does the balance of social relations change?

The year 2050 is a year of flux and it is not possible to answer these questions by visiting it at the moment. It is useful, however, to take such questions into consideration before leaving to visit 2050, because they challenge the foundations of our species as we know it today.

Another stratagem used by nature to multiply the chances of diffusion of our DNA and genes is to increase the production of certain hormones in pregnant women and mothers: these hormones amplify the predisposition to take care of children, both one's own and other people's. Thus, when oxytocin increases, so does the instinct to take care of third parties, especially if they are young and helpless. If gestation can no longer take place in the female body but in artificial uteri, then the changes in the body of women related to procreation no longer occur and for this reason, in 2050 births are artificially induced. But what does it mean to change this aspect of the human species? And what would happen if, over time, our body "forgot" how to develop this precious hormone associated with behaviours of trust and collaboration among humans?

BORDERLESS REPRODUCTION

Like many of the issues addressed in this book, reproduction has complications that go beyond the borders of a single state. The laws applied in this area vary greatly from country to country, creating a remarkable flow of travel and imports. Anyone wishing to undergo medical treatment or enhancement that is not allowed in their own country often decides to travel to get what they want. Some countries have made this a real business by competing to offer the most favourable conditions for patients or customers. This state of affairs is not new in 2050, although ease of movement has shortened the distances and made it the most common phenomenon.

But even if a country were to legalize treatment (e.g., artificial insemination), this would not necessarily eliminate travel or imports. Demand may exceed supply: What happens if there are not enough donors? There is a tendency to create a waiting list that can take up to two or three years. Another solution is to import eggs or sperm from other countries.

In 2018, Great Britain was heavily dependent on imports from countries such as Sweden and, after Brexit, it began to find itself facing serious shortages. That's why other countries or biobanks have given free rein to their creativity. In 2015, the Cryos International Sperm Bank was already offering free wellness holidays in France and Spain to women who agreed to donate eggs during their stay: this was to circumvent, for example, the Danish rules that did not allow the sale of eggs (which could instead be donated) unless there was minimum compensation, contrary to other EU countries and contrary to the rules on sperm donation. Another example dates back to 2003 when free holidays in Australia were offered to Canadian students who agreed to donate sperm every other day during their two-week stay. In this case the lack of local donors was caused by a new law coming into force at that time that prohibited sperm donors from remaining anonymous.

The perfect partner

In a hyper-connected world that is increasingly complex, always in a hurry, a world in which personal relationships are increasingly rare, how can we find the perfect partner with whom to share our hopes and dreams? Scientists and engineers have developed a series of inventions that try to answer this question. Before starting the search, however, you have to make an important choice: real partner, virtual reality partner or robot lover?

For those who choose the traditional way, the old courtship techniques no longer apply. The first encounter takes place more and more often between data and algorithms, which determine the existence of a match between people, examining their tastes, interests and desires. Only after this check is a first contact made, which can be either personal or in virtual reality. In the latter case, just wear a visor or a pair of laser-written contact lenses and you will find yourself face to face with your potential partner. Many, as a first step, choose the virtual option because the sensors of the virtual reality instruments, examining the dilation of the pupils and the heartbeats of both, immediately reveal whether there is an initial attraction. During the virtual appointment you can change location and enjoy a sunset by the sea, a walk in the countryside or a dinner on the top floor of a skyscraper overlooking the whole city. Thanks to a special suit and comfortable gloves equipped with neuromuscular electro-stimulators, you have the sensation of touching and manipulating objects and controlling the charged environment: you can hear the sound of the sea, the smell of flowers, the sensation of wet rain, the wind on your skin, heat and cold. In the best case, if Cupid fires his electronic arrow, you can also experience your first kiss in virtual format.

These virtual relationships, set up to help meet new people, are now widespread even among established couples living in different places: loving and maintaining a relationship at a distance is much easier since this technology exists.

To challenge the routine or try something new, those who connect to virtual reality can still decide to modify both their own appearance and that of their partner. Changing sex, race, height and body, it is possible to experiment with new situations and identities, each time choosing a different role.

LOVE AND VIDEO GAMES

The Nintendo DS *LovePlus* video game has been very popular in Japan since 2009. It's a real dating simulator in which you can choose from a range of possible digital companions.

Democratization of sex

Technology and medicine also play major roles from a social point of view, allowing people with serious physical, social and psychological problems to live a satisfying sexual life. Robots, virtual realities and medicines, in fact, can act on the senses and recreate experiences more and more similar to the reality they imitate. As in many other fields, there are innovations in the field of sex and relationships that go beyond mere care and enhance the possibilities of healthy human beings. Implantable technologies, genetic modifications, surgery and other modern techniques are increasingly used, not without controversy. Means such as 3D biostamps, medicines, drugs that act on desire or increase the sensations of pleasure with dopamine and serum: in 2050 there is a an answer to everything.

Robots in love

The great thing about asking someone "What is true love?" is that everyone will give a different answer. There are those who dream of an attractive partner, those who prefer a sensitive person, able to indulge and console them, those who want a fiery lover, those who want a companion with whom to share their passions. It is difficult, however, even with the help of artificial intelligence, to find a person who is able to fully reflect our expectations; for this reason, we often agree with those who tell us that, in order to love, we must be able to accept the defects of our partner. Companionship robots were created specifically to disprove this claim.

We have already warned travellers that 2050 humanoid robots are easily confused with human beings, and such robots trigger our natural empathy. They communicate, interact, respond, anticipate our desires, simulate emotions and sensations as if they were real humans. That's why, even when we know we're dealing with a robot, it's not always easy to manage our cares, our attention, our love. We forget in the blink of an eye we find ourselves in front of a machine that doesn't feel real emotions, that can't really love us. After all, when we are in love, we tend to reinterpret reality according to our wishes, even when it comes to other human beings.

Robots can take on the personality or aesthetic aspect that we prefer, either that of a famous movie star or that of an ex-girlfriend. In extreme cases, they may also impersonate deceased persons, provided that they have given their consent. If you have lost a friend, parent, girlfriend or husband, you are perfectly aware that the temptation to "bring them back

BOT BOY

The first "immortal dead" is called Roman Mazurenko and was programmed, after his physical death, by his best friend: Eugenia Kuyda. "He" dates back to 2016 and was the first real experiment where even those who had met the deceased when he was alive were satisfied, claiming that the impression given was that they were really chatting with Roman.[45]

to life" can seem irresistible. Well, in 2050, if you surf online, you may find yourself on a social network for the dead. On these strange websites you can find chatbots that converse and interact with each other and with the living, that connect in a sort of virtual cemetery that can also be visited through augmented or virtual reality. Maybe, having grown up in a world where death cannot be questioned, you know that our brain can forget, it can blur memories and alleviate pain (even if it cannot make them completely disappear); nevertheless, the process of mourning is a foundational part of our psychological make-up. So I'm leaving it up to you to think about how, in 2050, humans who grew up with similar tools always at their disposal were changed, just as society and the very concept of personal relationships may have fundamentally been disrupted. In any case, humanoid robots have had many positive impacts on society, including in terms of relationships: they have alleviated problems such as prostitution, slave and sex-slave trafficking, violence and paedophilia, not to mention their contribution to the almost total disappearance of sexually transmitted diseases such as AIDS. The synthetic fibre they are made of is resistant to bacteria and eliminates any risk of infection. If you think that you are only talking about a small part of the population who would be interested in such a relationship, it is worth noting that in 2050 it is considered normal to have sex with a machine.[46]

Beyond sex, however, the real revolution in the relationship between you and your machine is another: love. If you have time, go to Las Vegas or one of the other places where robot–human marriages are celebrated, and take part in one of these unmissable celebrations. It's a nice way to get in touch with the local culture.

Notes

[1] United Nations, Department of Economic and Social Affairs, Population Division, "World Population Prospects: Key Findings and Advance Tables", 2017 Revision, Working Paper No. ESA/P/WP/248, 2017.
[2] Istat, "Popolazione residente per stato civile", September 2018, available at istat.it.
[3] See T. de Chant's infographic, "The world population, concentrated", per-squaremile.com/, 18 January 2011.
[4] L. Clark, "Cyborgs like us", 2018, abstract available at https://www.thewire.ch/.
[5] See, among others, A. Bazzi, "Pacemaker messi fuori uso dagli hacker: rischio reale per i pazienti?", *Corriere della Sera*, 21 February 2018.

⁶ The acronym CRISPR-CAS9 stands for a protein complex which allows one to act in a precise way on a defective gene, either by inactivating it or by replacing it with a healthy gene. For this reason, it is often described as a technique that allows you to "cut and paste" DNA. For further information see the "Glossary of the future" at the end of this volume.

⁷ M. Gabanelli, A. Marinelli, "Genetica in garage: i rischi di modificare il dna in casa", *Corriere della Sera*, 2 October 2018.

⁸ Considering and combining the life expectancy data of robots and of humans with those of the expected production of robots, it is assumed that the trend leads to a significant increase in the number of robots used in the industry and in domestic and health services, to make some "of the company or for entertainment" (L. Streondj, "A home for robots or-else artilect war", joylifecoop.wordpress.com, 3 January 2016).

⁹ United Nations, "World Population Prospects".

¹⁰ United Nations, Department of Economic and Social Affairs, "World Urbanization Prospects", 2018 Revision, data set, population.un.org, 2018.

¹¹ D. Hoornweg and K. Pope, "Socioeconomic pathways and regional distribution of the world's 101 largest cities", Global Cities Institute Working Paper No. 4, 2014. For a comparison with the past, let's consider that in 1950 the main megacities were New York, Tokyo, London, Osaka and Paris; in 2010 they were Tokyo, Delhi, Mexico City, Shanghai and Sao Paulo.

¹² According to Bernard Foing, French scientist at European Space Agency (ESA) and Executive Director of the International Lunar Exploration Working Group (ILEWG), by 2050 there will be at least one thousand inhabitants on the Moon. These will no longer be just people who work on the satellite in the mines or refuelling space vehicles, but also their families, who are able to join them thanks to better livability of the space colonies ("Fly me to the Moon: For some, lunar village takes shape", phys.org, 22 September 2017).

¹³ South African entrepreneur and inventor, naturalized American Elon Musk, is famous for initiatives such as SpaceX, dedicated to civil space travel; Tesla Motors, with its self-driven electric cars and battery solutions for clean energy; PayPal, active in digital payment services; OpenAI, a non-profit organization for the dissemination of artificial intelligence; SolarCity, dedicated to solar energy; the Boring Company and Hyperloop, operating in the transport sector; Neuralink, for the enhancement of human cognitive skills through technology.

¹⁴ See for example I. Johnston, "Life on Mars: City of a million people could be built on Red Planet by 2062, says Elon Musk", *The Independent*, 22 June 2017.

¹⁵ According to some estimates, Hindi could reach the Chinese thanks to the great economic growth of the geographical area where it is the first language (see United Nations, "World Population Prospects").

¹⁶ Pew Research Center, "The future of world religions: Population growth projections, 2010–2050", pewforum.org, 2 April 2015 (in particular, "Religious Composition by Country, 2010–2050").

¹⁷ Yuval Noah Harari in his *Homo Deus. A Brief History of Tomorrow*, London, Harvill Secker, 2016.

¹⁸ A study published in *Nature* (C.S. Green, D. Bavelier, "Action video game modifies visual selective attention", *Nature*, 423 (6369), 29 May 2003) already

showed that those who played a lot of video games in their growth phase had also developed greater visual ability. Another study, from 2013 (A.J. Latham, L.L.M. Patston, L.J. Tippett, "The virtual brain: 30 years of video-game play and cognitive abilities", *Frontiers of Psychology*, 4, September 2013, 629), demonstrated further cognitive abilities developed in the same way.

[19] The term was coined in the 1980s and adopted by the winner of the Nobel Prize in Chemistry Paul Crutzen (see *Benvenuti nell'Antropocene. L'uomo ha cambiato il clima, la Terra entra in una nuova era*, Milan, Mondadori, 2005).

[20] G. Vince, "The Biosphere", in J. Al-Khalili (Ed.), *What's Next*, London, Profile Books, 2017.

[21] J.E.M. Watson, J.R. Allan *et al.*, "Protect the last of the wild", *Nature*, 563 (7729), November 2018, 27-30.

[22] M. Grooten, R.E.A. Almond (Eds.), *Living Planet Report 2018: Aiming Higher*, Gland, WWF, 2018.

[23] For more information see United Nations, "Concluding session to draft marine biodiversity treaty, conference president says environmental impact assessments will be reflected in instrument", un.org, 17 September 2018.

[24] The Commission is composed of twenty-five members and eleven member countries. For more information see www.ccamlr.org.

[25] Pia Mancini is now at the helm of Open Collective. Her 2014 TED talk, "How to upgrade democracy for the Internet era", received more than 1.2 million views.

[26] On the birth of DemocracyOS and its history see https://democracyos.org

[27] Open government platform active since 2017, in Italy: http://parliamentwatch.it/.

[28] WR, The Institute of digital democracy, "Cost of voting. Estimating the impact of online voting on public finance," 2017.

[29] https://info.vtaiwan.tw/.

[30] TV Series *Black Mirror*, Season 3, Episode 1, "Nosedive", 21 October 2016, available at netflix.com.

[31] D. Eggers, *The Circle*, New York, Alfred A. Kopf, 2013.

[32] For more information, see the interview "A. I. might run the world better than humans do" with Richard Dawkins, author, scientist and philosopher representing the neo-Darwinist movement, published on 23 September 2017 on the Big Think YouTube channel.

[33] Some exceptions are France, where at the time of the Revolution only half of the citizens spoke French, and Italy, where at the time of unification only 2.5% of the citizens spoke Italian.

[34] https://bitnation.co/.

[35] https://asgardia.space/en/.

[36] For more information see http://www.panarchy.org/.

[37] Austrian political philosopher and epistemologist, British naturalist who lived in the twentieth century. He was a fierce critic of totalitarianism and defender of democracy and the concept of an open society. The work we are referring to is *The Open Society and Its Enemies*, London, G. Routledge & Sons, 1945.

[38] Think, for example, of applications such as BlaBlaCar: traditional ownership of a car has been supplanted by a service based on an online platform that can

decentralize the use of the service, allowing anyone to give someone a ride in the car. Moreover, with the guarantee of feedback from other users, it is easy for both employers and passengers to trust even strangers.

[39] F. Xiang, "AI will spell the end of capitalism", *Washington Post*, 3 May 2018.

[40] S. Petrucciani, *Marx*, Rome, Carocci, 2009.

[41] As Marx himself pointed out in *The Capital* and as recalled by S. Petrucciani in his *Marx*.

[42] Noam Chomsky is a linguist at the Massachusetts Institute of Technology, philosopher, historian of communication and great scholar of the most varied disciplines. For further information, please refer to his website: https://chomsky.info/.

[43] P. Coelho, *Eleven Minutes*, New York, HarperCollins Publishers, 2004.

[44] J. Gallagher, "Same-sex mice have babies", bbc.com, 11 October 2018.

[45] C. Newton, "Speak, Memory. When her best friend died, she rebuilt him using artificial intelligence", www.theverge.com, October 2016.

[46] D. Levy, *Love and Sex with Robots: The Evolution of Human–Robot Relationships*, New York, HarperCollins, 2009.

2 Practical Information

The climate

There's no point in beating around the bush: the climate in 2050 is much more extreme than the one we're used to today. The surface temperature has increased by two degrees Celsius since 1950 (in large cities it is said to be four or five degrees) and the global sea level has risen by thirty centimetres.[1] If you think that this is not important or that it is enough to equip yourself with the right clothing you are wrong: the impacts of such a change are many and of different types.

First of all, it is crucial to remember that a large number of past revolutions and wars were caused, to some degree, by the scarcity of food products, caused in turn by famine and climate change. Any examples? On 8 June 1783, the Icelandic volcano Laki, still active and monitored for its explosive power, began to erupt, opening 130 craters and continuing unabated for the next eight months. The eruption had more or less direct effects throughout Europe, causing massacres of livestock due to poisoning from soil contamination, thousands of deaths and weather anomalies. The amount of sulphur dioxide emitted during the eruption was three times higher than that emitted by European industry in 2006. The effects were felt also in France, towards the end of the eighteenth century, when great climatic changes took place which had a heavy impact on agricultural production: first an enormous overproduction, disastrous for the economy because it caused the fall of prices and the consequent impoverishment of the farmers, then drought, freezing winters and very bad summers.

The tipping point was reached in 1788 when a violent hailstorm destroyed the crops. It goes without saying that, in 1789, the people were angry, hungry and impoverished. And we all know the story of the

French Revolution. The eruption of a volcano in Iceland, therefore, can be counted among the main causes of one of the most important events in Western history.

Any more recent examples? The 2008 food crisis was one of the reasons for the fall of the Haitian government, while the increase in food prices in 2011 certainly contributed to the start of the Arab Spring.

Now let's try to imagine the consequences of the climate changes taking place in the twenty-first century. Summarizing and simplifying (Figure 13), we can gain an idea of some of the combined effects of climate change: the melting of ice reserves, droughts and floods, extreme and more difficult to foresee climatic events, rising sea levels all affect the most precious resource on our planet: water. The effect on water is central, especially if superimposed on other issues of 2050 that affect it, such as population growth and globalization, which cause increased water demand and cause intensive exploitation and pollution of groundwater.

Figure 13 Concatenated effects of global warming

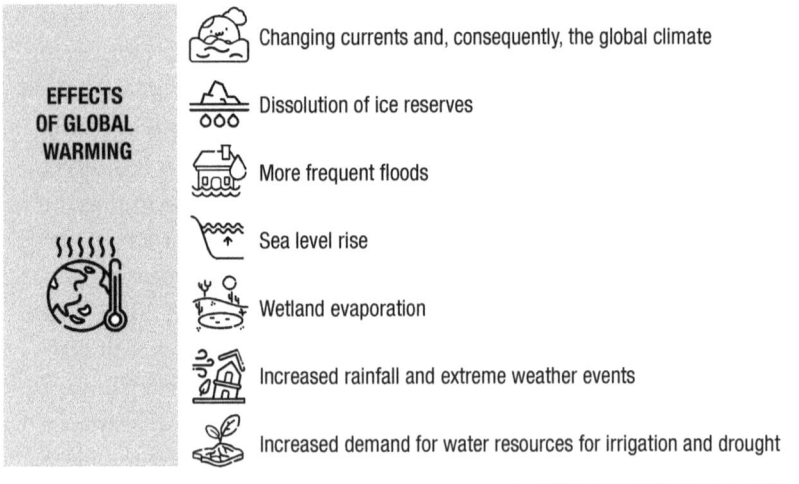

And so, in 2050, migratory flows have increased, caused not only by the search for better education, work and escape from difficult political and social situations, but also by floods, droughts, rains, monsoons and other natural disasters that caused a crisis affecting many sectors, particularly agriculture.

As a result of climate change, the Nordic countries can take advantage of a climate more favourable to certain crops, which has led to a change in the balance of the global trade for this reason. If you love winter sports, in 2050 you will not have much chance to practice them in natural environments. Many of the ski resorts we are used to are no longer viable, because there is so little snow.

Another area particularly affected by climate change is the Arctic. In summer, it is increasingly free of ice, so much so that people can exploit new trade routes: the fastest way to connect Asia and the West passes right through there. This shock in the Arctic Ocean has great consequences for the global climate. To understand what happens we have to explain the phenomenon of albedo, that is, the intensity with which a surface reflects the sun's rays: in Figure 14 you will notice that ice and water have extremely different degrees of albedo: the former at 90 per cent and the latter at 10 per cent.

Figure 14 The phenomenon of the albedo

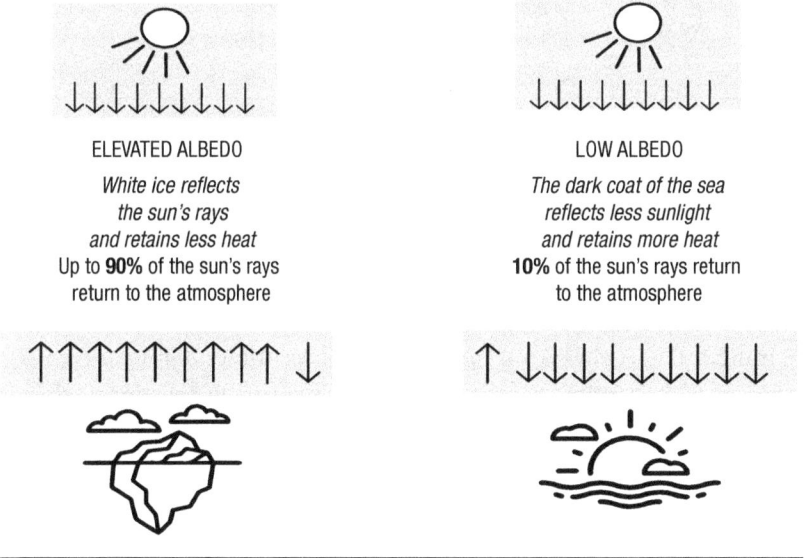

This is important because when the ice of the Arctic Ocean melts due to global warming, changing the degree of albedo over a very large area, temperatures inevitably change too. The sea absorbs 90 per cent of the sun's rays and transforms them into heat; the thin ice mass that forms in winter, on the other hand, functions as a thermal blanket and maintains the temperature of the water unchanged. Because of the melting of the ice, therefore, the climate becomes milder not only in the Arctic, but also in large areas of the planet that are affected by currents from this area (Figure 15).

Figure 15 Albedo combined with climate change

The melting of sea ice increases the percentage of surface area with lower degrees of albedo and retains more heat

Increases water temperature

Mellower climate and changes in currents affect the climate around the world and end up feeding the process itself

It is important to note that the melting of the Arctic sea ice does not raise the sea level, like other phenomena, as a result of the Archimedes principle. You can easily test this principle by immersing an ice cube in a bucket of water; since the density of the ice is lower than the density of the water, when it melts the level will not increase: a cubic centimetre of ice weighs less than a cubic centimetre of water. This interests us because in the case of the North Pole we have a large amount of ice that floats directly on the surface of the sea and that, when melting, does not make the sea level increase . In the case of the South Pole, on the contrary, we have a continent, Antarctica, where the ice is above the ground; the ice therefore melts less quickly because it does not suffer the effect of the heat retained by the sea, but when it melts it increases the water level.

It is important to remember that another phenomenon also occurs (albeit with minor effects compared to the above): the thermal expansion of the oceans. In this case, the temperature increase that interests us is that of the air, which is able to heat the water by increasing its volume: in fact, the space between the molecules increases as a result of the heat.

BLUE GOLD

It is now clear: the fate of 2050 is linked to water resources. This is what a scientific article published in 2018 also claims.[2] It shows which areas will be most at risk of conflicts related to water resources (Figure 16). However, the article also proposes solutions so as not to risk tensions degenerating into conflicts.

Figure 16 Global distribution of the probability of hydro-political problems developing among the main transboundary basins

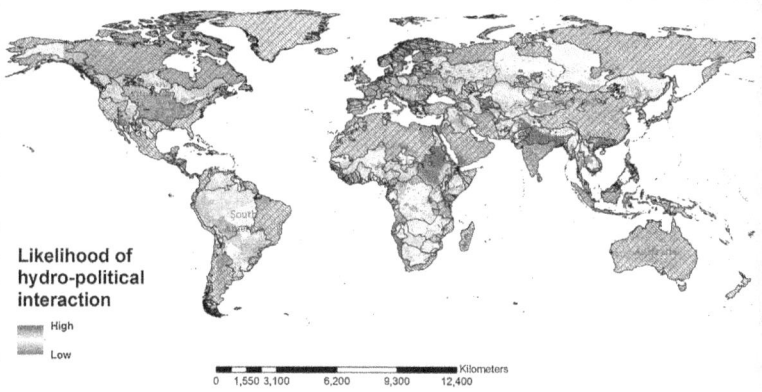

Source: F. Franzosi *et al.*, «An innovative approach to the assessment of hydro-political risk», cit., https://doi.org/10.1016/j.gloenvcha.2018.07.001 (Creative Commons Attribution License (CC BY)).

Animals and nature

In your travels in 2050 you will encounter new forms of life, not only among humans but also among the other animals of our beautiful planet. Scientists, starting from the DNA filaments available and exploiting genetics and technological systems, have succeeded in bringing back to life several extinct species and in creating completely new ones using genetic recombination techniques or artificial fertilization.[3] Do not be surprised, therefore, if during your visit you come across animals studied only in the old history books. If you would like to learn more about the subject, a good idea is to spend some of your time visiting one of the many zoos dedicated to the species of the past.[4]

UNICORNS AND OTHER ANIMALS

In the face of the great possibilities introduced by technologies and advances in genetic editing, important ethical dilemmas arise. Several researchers are creating in the laboratory species of "mixed" animals, real chimeras. Animals that in the past were considered fantastic or imaginary have now become reality, thanks the recombination of DNA.
Genetic recombination consists of removing a DNA sequence from one organism and implanting it into another, actually creating organisms that would not exist in nature. Since it was invented, numerous experiments have been carried out, for example creating bacteria that produce human insulin and fluorescent plants as a result of genes from jellyfish. But now in some countries scientists are going much further and are working on the creation of new animals, such as unicorns and dragons. Public opinion is divided: on the one hand are those in favour and those simply curious and, on the other, those who believe that it is unethical to play with DNA and with life forms for a variety of reasons, not least that we do not know the consequences of similar experiments in the medium and long term nor if the animal thus created could be exposed to suffering due to the artificial modifications and their evolutions.

Chimeras

In 2050, the term "chimera" recurs frequently and it will be useful to clarify in which sense it is used. In the meantime, we can define it as an animal formed by parts of what in nature are different animals. In Greek mythology it was a scary monster. In the field of research and health it is "simply" a being that is born from a mix of different DNAs or that presents characteristics that are not natural to it. Either way, it is a beast that has been around for a long time!

Figure 17 Examples of controversial past chimeras

1988	1997	2000	2000
SCID-hu Mouse This mouse, created at Stanford by Irv Weissman to study the human immune system, contains human genes within its DNA.	**Ear Mouse** Created by Charles A. Vacanti, this mouse had an ear-shaped cartilage structure on its back. The study that led to its creation was part of the research framework for the creation of organs in the laboratory. In this case, there was no DNA manipulation.	**Human Neuron Mouse** Human Neuron Mouse The idea of inserting human neurons into the interior of a mouse brain was the basis of one of the first famous experiments that sparked the debate on chimeras, and was discussed at length after Weissman proposed it in 2000.	**Sunrise** the fluorescent rabbit The artist Eduardo Kac created Alba by modifying its DNA so that this contained a gene typical of jellyfish that can turn the rabbit fluorescent green.

In 2018 the case of what was called by the newspapers "sheep-human hybrids" became famous, unleashing the imagination of the public. The study in question aimed to explore the possibility of making up for the shortage of human organs for transplantation by creating human embryos within other animals. After the pig in 2017 it was the turn of the sheep in 2018. In both cases the embryo with human material on board was blocked in its development after twenty-eight days but the operation nevertheless raised a fierce ethical discussion regarding the possibility, one day, of developing this technique. Other cases of chimeras are all those which have undergone an operation involving the implantation of pig or bovine heart valves to ensure the functioning of a sick human heart.

Effects of climate on animals

The most attentive will certainly also notice the movements that many animal species are making, driven by climate change. This is no news, but a trend already known: a 2003 study found that every decade many animals move their territory just over six kilometres towards the poles and six metres in altitude.[5] These same animals are also changing their reproductive and hibernation habits, which are moving four days earlier each decade.[6]

Just like humans, the animals of 2050 try to adapt to the new environment: there are species which change over several generations and others which, against all expectations, creating new hybrids, as was already discovered in 2006 when a *grolar* bear, born from the union of a grizzly bear and a polar bear, was discovered.[7]

A new role for animals?

Thanks to technological and scientific progress, animals, in addition to preserving biodiversity, are beginning to play, in relation to humans, an increasingly domestic role. In 2050, the tendency is to use animals less and less for food or scientific experiments: meat,[8] protein and its derivatives can now be produced in the laboratory at affordable prices, as well as everything needed to test drugs or other scientific innovations. That's why it's not unusual to come across a cow in a public garden or a pig in a kindergarten courtyard: these animals are cared for and pampered, in the belief that the more healthy and serene their life, the tastier the meat obtained in the laboratory from their cells.

The care of pets is often supported by *bot-pet-sitters* who look after them and monitor their health. On rainy days, or when the owners are unable to do so, they also walk the animals.

Many animals are also *smart*: thanks to small chips under the skin that amplify their capabilities and allow them to better interact with human beings. Mechanical prostheses, which are often invisible, correct malformations and possible physical defects, with the result that even animals who are victims of accidents and operations can live a healthy life. Warning: if you come across a dog that looks shy and harmless, think twice before caressing him: he could be reprogrammed as a defence dog and behind that mild appearance may have the strength of a grizzly bear.

COWBORG AND OTHER ANIMALS

Are there more human cyborgs or animal cyborgs? In 2020, the latter is true as implanting chips to track and detect vital signs in pets, such as dogs, or in farm animals, such as cows, is common practice. In 2050, however, thanks to the decrease in intensive herds and the parallel increase in human cyborgs, the proportion is reversing.

Religious rites

If you want to breathe the culture of 2050 to the full, you can attend some of the rituals of the most practised religions. These rituals are very different from those to which we are accustomed in 2020: if you are among those who think that technology and religion cannot get along, get ready to think again. You will come across Masses celebrated completely in virtual reality, augmented reality shows and immersive and touching rituals. During Christian services, for example, readings of the Gospel are replaced by virtual experiences, which, by allowing us to relive in the first person all the crucial moments of the life of Jesus, such as the crucifixion and the betrayal of Judas, create a very strong empathy and a feeling of true unification with the body of Christ. Offers are made with virtual money – so do not try to donate coins or banknotes because they would not be accepted.

If, since the Middle Ages, the Church has made extensive use of the "robotic", creating automatic mechanisms that allowed statues to move under the impetus of apparent divine forces, in 2050 special effects are the order of the day. It is not a matter of deception: the technologies are all well known and are not used to convince unbelievers or fool the naive, but to heighten the feelings of believers, increase empathy and help them remember the principles underlying the religion. For this reason, each religion adopts different rites and technologies: if you want to get a more complete and in-depth idea, the advice is to visit the sacred places of each.

No language barriers

In a 2014 Technology Entertainment Design (TED) talk,[9] Nicholas Negroponte stated:[10] "My prediction is that we are going to ingest information. You're going to swallow a pill and know English. You're going to swallow a pill and know Shakespeare . . ."[11] In 2050, thanks to the development of biotechnologies, his vision has almost become reality, but it is not the only way to learn about things that exist in the future.

NEGROPONTE FORECASTS

Negroponte is famous for his highly accurate future predictions. Let's name a few:

- the possibility of buying books and magazines online (judged insane in 1995 by Clifford Stoll, journalist for *Newsweek*);
- the evolution of TV into a new digital tool capable of communicating with a computer, planned for in 1985;
- the use of touch technologies, now the basis of tablets and mobile phones, but opposed, in 1970s, by those who were convinced that the fingers would dirty the screens and prevented reading what was underneath.

So don't worry about the language problem: as soon as you arrive in 2050, you will be able to supply yourself with various tools that will help you to understand the foreign languages fully.

The main features of the project are the following: (a) the number of dialects, (b) the local vocabulary and linguistic changes over the last thirty years. One of these tools is represented by the pills imagined by Negroponte, but if the idea of swallowing a language seems too odd to you, you can simply wear earphones connected to the network that translate all the idioms simultaneously, and special glasses (or contact lenses) that can do the same with the written texts. Just look at a word or phrase and you'll see it translated into your language.

Food

Food and nutrition have never been more important than in 2050. This year, human beings are taking action to solve the problem of hunger and malnutrition in a world where well over 9 billion people live. While the population has exploded, agriculture is being put to the test by the effects of climate change, resulting in desertification, erosion, loss of biodiversity and reduced natural availability of uncontaminated freshwater. Humans have understood that it is more necessary than ever to learn to feed themselves using sustainable production methods, which can decrease air pollution and soil overexploitation.

A new agricultural revolution

In the eighteenth century, the development of new agricultural technologies in Western Europe marked the beginning of a series of slow changes that gave rise to what many scholars call the "agricultural revolution". The result was an increase in production capacity, to meet the needs of a population increase of 40 per cent. New technologies, technologies already known for centuries but never applied extensively, association and integration of breeding and agriculture: these were the key elements of change, which led to the birth of industrial production and the creation of a larger market.

From the mid-nineteenth century on, states began to understand the importance of technological development and to invest in research and development and in the creation of agricultural institutes, thus grafting in a series of new changes that, since then, have continued to evolve.

In the middle of the twentieth century, moreover, the so-called *green revolution*, combining the availability of artificial fertilizers with high-yield agriculture, allowed billions of people who, otherwise, would not have enough to eat, to be fed.

However, scholars have not always agreed on the use of the term "agricultural revolution",[12] which is often used in too general a way. In 2050, however, everyone seems to be converging towards one point: we are facing a historical moment that is worthy of being called the "new agricultural revolution".

Enhanced delicacies

For lovers of good food, 2050 is a destination rich in opportunities and gastronomic surprises. Following our advice you can try all these novelties and give your palate an unforgettable experience.

Don't make the mistake of thinking of food as just a way to indulge or to appease hunger; in 2050 the reasons for eating have multiplied: you eat to treat a disease, to better prepare for a sport or physical activity, to change your mood, for beauty and for preventative health measures.

Culinary engineering

Behaviour, information, data: in 2050, food is only conceived, prepared and cooked after analysing the individual characteristics and objectives of the person who will eat it. According to our DNA, our mood, our tastes and our possible intolerances, we can choose, at any time and place, the option that best suits us. An artificial intelligence that is synchronized with our devices will advise us on a personalized diet, reminding us how many calories we need to take to meet our daily goals, avoid intoxication, prevent allergies and keep ourselves healthy. During the trip we will be able to eat hypotensive grapes, anti-tumor bread, fruit drinks with immunological prophylaxis and flu-free meat.

Thanks to big data, genomics and computer science, it is possible to analyse each type of food at a molecular level, identify the peptides that have beneficial effects for humans and thus modify existing foods to give them new characteristics. If the fear is that such intelligent foods may lose something in terms of taste and appearance, don't worry: if you visit restaurants, shops, touring car distributors, 3D printers (in 2050 you'll also be printing food!) and supermarkets, you'll immediately realize that the food of 2050 does have shapes, colours and scents that are different from those we're used to, but this only makes them tastier, thanks to the many possibilities of personalizing them. Fish protein in the form of cakes, cakes in tablets, medicine-ice cream, grasshopper chips are just some of the foods we are dealing with in 2050. But beware: with this variety of shapes and colours it is easy to get confused. To always be sure of what we are going to taste, it is advisable to equip ourselves with a portable device that, exploiting hyperspectral waves and artificial intelligence, allows us to scan the food and verify that all the ingredients are to our liking: it will be enough to bring the sensor to the plate and in a few seconds we will know what we are going to taste, when it has been cooked, what is inside and predict if we will like it. By analysing raw materials such as meat, eggs, cheese, fruit or vegetables, we will be able to trace where they were produced, when and with what techniques, and retrace through videos, photos and graphs their entire cycle of production and recycling.

This is possible thanks to new rules that ensure all agricultural and food products can be fully traced, in order to avoid the waste of the past. In 2018, for example, one third of the world's food production was literally thrown away, increasing pollution in the disposal process. Another problem that is being overcome in 2050 is the decline in biodiversity. Consider that in 2018, 75 per cent of food was generated by only twelve plants and five animal species. As there are 300,000 edible plants, you can imagine how many possibilities are being explored in the 2050 diet.[13]

TRACED NEEDS

In some countries, in order to combat waste and the unequal distribution of food between rich and poor, control systems have been introduced, not without some controversy, linked to special wearable devices and based on blockchain technology. The reasoning is simple: those who keep to their daily need for resources are rewarded with lower prices, those who invest are able to decide to eat and drink more than necessary, but pay higher prices for the excess, thereby economically supporting the poorest.
There is no shortage of controversy over how this system curtails the privacy and freedom of individuals, but it is still too early to evaluate the results of ongoing trials and judge whether it is worth continuing the experiment.

Targeted diets

In the future there are a myriad of different food movements, including those supported by vegans, vegetarians, paleodietists (who eat only what humans ate 15,000 years ago), raw foodists (who eat only raw food), fruitarians (remember Steve Jobs?), fisharians (who are vegetarian but also eat fish), breatharians (who strive to eat as little as possible), insectarians (who feed exclusively on insects) and cannibals.[14] For each of these diets, there are ad hoc food programmes and tailor-made recipes that you can try. It is important to note that the term "diet" in 2050 has taken on a much more complete meaning than that used in 2020: it is now clear that our body evolves according to the substances we ingest so the diets of the future are designed to modify our DNA and the colonies of microbes that live in our bodies, to aid our general health and prevent disease.

Restaurants and robots

Our culinary tour must begin in one of the many automated restaurants scattered across the planet. Once we have crossed the threshold, we are welcomed by a robot waiter who accompanies us to the table. Forget paper menus and ordering by voice: we can consult and order the dishes directly from the hologram screen on our table and decide when they will be ready. If we want a drink or a bottle of wine, a simple click provides these; in more advanced restaurants, it may be enough simply to think of something because brainwave detection systems process the order. If the available drinks are not to our liking, we can ask for the service "Soda do-it-yourself": after having selected the ingredients and the relative quantities, a bot will assist us to avoid creating drinks that are too sweet, too bitter or incompatible with our bodies.

Via a small screen next to our chair we can observe what the robotic cooks prepare in the kitchen. Meals are presented by service robots or emerge from a small opening in each table, which is connected directly to the kitchen. In some rooms, however, you can pick up your order from a large wall distributor called the *food wall* (or send your own personal robot to pick it up for you).

In many of these restaurants, the ambience is adapted to the customers' needs. The lights, music, temperature and images on the table and on the screens around the walls change on the basis of complex calculations that analyse the mood of all diners and create the perfect atmosphere for every need.

At the end of the meal you can simply stand up and leave because the payment is automatic, thanks to facial recognition devices. Remember that no tips are left here: the workers are all robots and the service is included in the price.

CULINARY HABITATS

In 2050, premises will use augmented reality to offer more personalized experiences. Not all restaurants are designed like today's and individual rooms are quite common. There are different options available for each table (for individuals or groups) where, according to the choice of the clients, relaxing themes (for example "tropical beach"), or adventurous, spatial or much more immersive experiences take place.

Important: Terms and conditions of use

Automated restaurants of the future make extensive use of artificial intelligence, biometric and DNA analysis. Before entering, therefore, let's make sure we understand all the terms of service, so as not to have any unpleasant surprises. All these data reveal a great deal of information about our state of health and our private and working life. If we grant access to this information, the data controllers will know everything about us. Unfortunately, not all countries on the planet have adhered to the rules on privacy and restaurants may not inform us about their possible data collection systems; for this reason it is advisable to use online platforms and blockchain to check restaurant policies and customer reviews: if the reviews have the appropriate "biometric" symbol, it means that they have been drawn up automatically by means of restaurant surveys, if instead they bear the "human" symbol they have been entered manually by customers and, probably, the restaurant does not use the data unless expressly authorized by the customers themselves.

To understand the value of personal information, it is sufficient to note that in some restaurants, discounts of up to 100 per cent are offered to those who authorize the collection of their data and its transfer to third parties. If you believe that the information contained in your genetic code is not particularly "personal", remember that as early as 2017, starting from simple DNA, some researchers managed to trace people's social profiles, while some software could gain enough information about the physical appearance of an individual to create special 3D models very similar to the original,[15] and scientists can even clone a living entities, from sheep to chimpanzees.

Secret ingredient: Humanity

There are also some chains of restaurants with a "human" touch, where all the service staff are real human beings. These are top-level actors, ready to offer an unforgettable entertainment experience. Since it is rare not to have a service robot, the cost of human servers is very high and the experience is considered to be an exclusive one. In this case tips are welcome and can be up to 100 per cent of the value of the meal. Having a human worker entails very high costs for the restaurant, and the burden of paying contributions and taxes derived from labour income falls entirely on the client, who is more or less obliged to tip.

Food in 3D

If you prefer a snack on the fly over a dinner or full lunch, try the 3D food dispensers: present at any street corner and active around the clock, these coloured boxes allow you to print and create any type of dish in a moment. The food characteristics and ingredients are totally customizable, as are the temperature, quantity and quality of the raw materials.

3D food-printing machines are now widespread in almost every home and in most hotel rooms, so if you don't feel like going out one night, you can try out these tailor-made services that, in addition to snacks, can prepare full meals. If, on the other hand, you wish to feed yourself, you can choose an apartment with a kitchen: even if almost all food is pre-packaged or pre-cooked, there are many people who still enjoy the pleasure of cooking.

GIY (GROW IT YOURSELF)

A new fashion is taking hold among the nostalgics of the past: it is not uncommon to come across recipes, instructions, tutorials and robots dedicated to teaching one how to grow, grow, prepare and cook food at home. There are also single-plant robots that monitor all the important cultivation data. Urban gardens, for example, are controlled and maintained by algorithms that deal with the entire cycle of cultivation of fruit and vegetables: from sowing to pruning, to the delivery of the first fruits directly into our refrigerator. Domesticated animals (cows, sheep, pigs) live happily in public gardens, or in the outdoor spaces of schools and houses, in exchange for the donation of some of their cells for the creation of in vitro meat in the laboratory; it is also common to have small grasshopper farms in one's garden. In addition, in all major supermarkets we will find, in the form of special wafers to be inserted in the instruments of the house, the chemical elements necessary for both the creation of custom foods and their preservation. It is as simple as making coffee or making popcorns in the microwave hoven.

Supermarkets in 2050

You may find it hard to recognize them, but in 2050 supermarkets still exist: forget the shelves though! Once you enter these huge buildings, you will find yourself immersed in an open environment where computer visuals, sensors, artificial intelligence and deep learning create a unique shopping experience, designed to entertain and interact with customers. Supermarkets have become the place where you can also go to meet other people, make friends and learn about all the latest food and wine news.

As soon as we cross the threshold, a robot will tell us which of the products we use most often is on offer and if there are new products compatible with our tastes. If we have to organize a dinner, he will advise us on the best wine and ingredients, not only on the basis of what we want to cook, but also on what our guests usually buy. You will find exclusively functional food for sale: tailor-made and timed for each segment of the population – women, men, the elderly, children, sportspeople and students.

If we try to take a product into our hands, a hologram will appear next to us with all the product's main nutritional values imprinted on it. Just touch a courgette to know its complete biography: where it was born, who cultivated it, what substances it has fed on, how long it has been on sale. To reduce pollution and waste, the packaging is reduced to a minimum and all the materials used are recyclable and come from renewable sources; most of the packaging, moreover, is edible and 100 per cent biodegradable. We can thus choose, from dozens of different types of packaging, the one with the best taste. Once we have completed our shopping, we can simply leave the supermarket. Artificial intelligence systems will recognize the images of the food and our identity for the purposes of payment. For the lazy, there is a system of autonomous drones or robots, which, within fifteen minutes, will deliver the shopping to them.

Supermarkets are subject to the same privacy considerations as restaurants: always pay attention to the terms and conditions before choosing a service.

Dishes not to be missed

All visitors returning from 2050 agree on one thing: the food and dishes tasted are worth the trip on their own. And we're sure you'll say the same thing, too.

Much of the food available in 2050 is the result of genetic reworking: thanks to recent advances in GMO (genetically modified food), fruits and vegetables are healthier, look better and last longer. Modified seeds have led to the creation of new species: cube-shaped tomatoes (easier and more flexible storage), multiform courgettes, apples that do not bruise, redder strawberries, rice that does not expire. All without sacrificing taste. Harmful food components have been removed: wheat is produced without the skin harmful to digestion, tobacco is deprived of the carcinogenic substances triggered by the combustion of cigarettes.

However, not all available food has similar characteristics, both because of a cost problem and because there are movements that challenge the application of genomics in the field of food. These groups argue that it is not ethically correct to change nature and that we do not yet know enough about the effects on our bodies of such enhanced foods.

New agricultural techniques and varieties of food

From field to laboratory: this could be the title of a documentary on the new agricultural methods used and applied in 2050, methods that have transformed farmers into real engineer-scientists.

The combination of artificial intelligence, robotics, biotechnology and nanotechnology ensures the best conditions for the development and growth of a food product – monitoring its evolution, and controlling its taste, size, consistency and other characteristics that make it healthy and delicious – are replicated. The drones monitor the fields and distribute, in a targeted manner, products necessary to protect the plants from possible contamination; artificial intelligence systems constantly monitor the state of fruit and vegetables and calculate how much water, light and manure are needed. Agricultural soils are optimized and are used to improve the quality of the soil.

The algorithms are able to make accurate weather forecasts and schedule each production cycle. The use of seawater greenhouses also makes it possible to exploit waste land.

Nanotechnologies and biotechnologies allow seeds to be modified, giving them characteristics that they would not have in nature and sensors able to communicate their state of health.

OPEN LABORATORIES

If we have aroused your curiosity, do not miss visiting one of the many agricultural laboratories. Those that are located in the main cities allow you to take guided tours and taste some typical dishes in the restaurant area. Of all of them, we recommend that you take a look at those that apply hydroponic culture: here the plants are not cultivated using soil but a solution of water and nutritional substances. This technique allows a higher yield, reduces water consumption, optimizes light and heat and allows better control of potential plant diseases, because bacteria are more difficult to reproduce above ground.

INTRUSION INTO SEATTLE'S AGRICULTURAL LABORATORIES

A group of thieves entered Seattle's agricultural laboratory last night, using special 3D-printed silicone masks. The masks seem to have been designed by copying the physical traits and characteristics of the scientists who work in the laboratory, and succeeded in deceiving the facial recognition system.

The police came to this conclusion after initially interrogating the scientists themselves; but a few checks of the data concerning their movements recorded in their devices were enough to prove that they were not to blame.

It is not yet clear what the thieves took.

FOILED HACKER ATTACK ON CORN CROPS

Hackers wanted to ruin the crops of the next four years with an attack of global scope, but the Chinese cyber police got wind of this in time and yesterday afternoon carried out a maxi-arrest of twenty individuals, both human and robot, who were involved.

Proteins, proteins, proteins

In 2050, plant proteins are increasingly used as the basis for most food created in laboratories. There is an almost unlimited range of such food, but above anything else it is worth tasting artificial eggs: both hardboiled and scrambled, and as a basis for mayonnaise. You will discover that they cannot be distinguished from natural eggs! If you are nostalgic, you can taste products, such as mayonnaise, made from the proteins of eggs created in the laboratory, rather than from vegetables.

Thanks to their ability to grow rapidly and their intrinsic richness in vitamins, minerals and antioxidants, algae are also used in a myriad of delicious recipes. Not to mention that they can be used to produce feed, plastics, pharmaceuticals, oils and biofuels. That's why you'll find extensive algae cultivation all over the world.

Algae and plants are also used for the production of fish and molluscs. If you order a cocktail of green shrimp, you can enjoy the same taste as fresh fish, with the same proteins and unsaturated fat content, but without cholesterol and or toxins caused by sea pollution. Fish and shellfish do not now cause intolerances: even allergic people can eat them. So make sure you always check the ingredients on the menu, because you can take advantage of the fact that in 2020 you will not be able to eat such food.

Despite the widespread use of aquatic organisms created in the laboratory, it is also possible to buy and order real fish: new discoveries about their metabolism and the use of innovative aquaculture techniques has made it possible to implement sustainable, biodiversity-friendly farming systems in the open sea, capable of producing tastier and more ecological fish, and of eliminating the use and production of polluting substances altogether. In the case of fish, too, however, the in vitro cultivation of proteins can be chosen. Fish cells can be used to grow delicious fillets without the need to end the life of the original fish.

Among the various fish dishes available, try the jellyfish at least once: in 2050 their proliferation is no longer seen as a problem, but as a delicious opportunity, and jellyfish are considered a refined ingredient, the basis of many recipes. The abundance of bioactive compounds makes this one of the most popular and widespread food sources.

In vitro animal proteins

In 2050, therefore, animal proteins are produced in the laboratory both for food purposes and (as we will see in the section on "Shopping and services") for industrial purposes. After all, with the increase in the population and the improvement in the economic and social conditions of some countries, meat consumption has doubled compared to the first decades of the century and sustainable alternatives had to be found.[16]

The technique has existed for quite some time, as the very first experiments date back to the 1970s, when Russell Ross managed to cultivate some muscle fibres. In the early 2000s, NASA and NSR/Touro Applied BioScience Research Consortium experiments created turkey meat and goldfish fillets in the laboratory. The process was structured in the following decade, up to the turning point of 2013, the year of the first public demonstration with the tasting of a synthetic hamburger.[17] Since then, giant steps have been made both in terms of cost reduction and in terms of yield and taste: the first in vitro burger cost €220,000 at the time and did not even taste nice.

In 2050 the problem of taste has been fixed and the technique is widely used. There is in fact no animal protein that cannot be cultivated in vitro: from cattle, sheep, fish, poultry, eggs and much more, to the point of reaching, not without controversy, human beings. So how do you choose between plant and animal proteins? The main difference is that the vegetable protein is fat-free, while the artificial one has some aromas, added in the laboratory, which make it smell nicer. The taste, however, is practically identical. Both methods make it possible to avoid the intensive exploitation and slaughter of animals, with real benefits for the environment: greenhouse gas emissions and the waste of water (one cow burger = two hundred litres of water) have been drastically reduced.

If you decide to taste synthetic animal protein products, you can choose the animal from which the starting cells were taken. Several restaurants have an outdoor area where chickens, cattle, rabbits and pigs roam freely and children can interact with them: just select the one you like and, in a few minutes, you can enjoy an excellent steak or a stew cooked with the meat previously produced by its cells.

Figure 18 How to create a steak in the laboratory

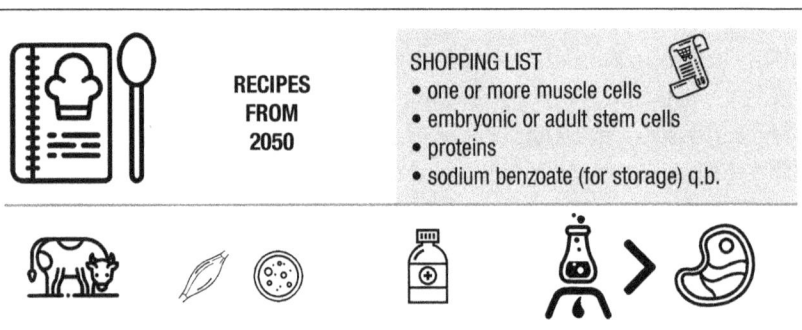

| Choose your favourite animal: you can choose the one with the most exciting life, viewing its history on your device. | Take a muscle cell and embryonic or adults stem cells. | Nourish the cell with proteins that activate and increase tissue growth. | Place in a bioreactor and start. Let the process continue for the desired time (for example, in two months a pig cell can produce 5,000 tons of meat, so be careful not to lose the keys to the laboratory!). |

The strangest dining experience that you will encounter in 2050, however, is the presence of controversial restaurants that offer dishes based on human artificial meat: much sought after, these places allow one to eat meat created using the cells of famous people, such as actors, musicians or space explorers. The sale of human artificial meat is only legal in some countries, but public opinion appears to be changing, given the restaurants' great successes and the increasing number of bookings. It is not altogether unlikely, therefore, that in the next few decades the law may change: after all, to obtain such meat, no human being is hurt. If you are intrepid and curious and want to try cannibalism, our advice is to book well in advance: the waiting lists of these restaurants can be as long as sixteen months.

Returning to more traditional choices, if you are a connoisseur of dairy products, try the milk-based cheeses created in the laboratory with GMO yeast cultures: you will be delighted by the softness of the mozzarella and the rich flavour of the mature cheeses.

Waiter, there's a bug in my plate!

In the 2050 food and wine tour you can't forget to taste the most popular food on the planet: insects, such as locusts, grasshoppers, crickets and ants. These animals not only do not contain cholesterol and saturated fats but, on the contrary, are rich in proteins, minerals and vitamins, which is why they have quickly conquered tables around the world. Furthermore, the spread of insects has been favoured by the advantages that their production guarantees in comparison to that of traditional breeding. Due to their small size they consume less resources than cows and other large animals and can easily be bred on a large scale. In particular, it is useful to note that in the case of insects the ratio between the total mass of the creature (and the need for nourishment) and the edible mass of the same is much more efficient than that of cattle, pigs and, to a lesser extent, poultry. In the case of crickets, for example, 80 per cent of the animal is edible, while in the case of cattle we eat only 40 per cent of its mass.[18]

You can grill the insects, fry them in a pan with a little oil and chilli, or crunch them as a snack to appease a sudden burst of hunger. Finally, the insects are often ground and utilized as flour, used in a variety of recipes, from bread to pasta, from cakes to desserts.

Minimal solutions

If you prefer to devote your time to cultural visits and travel, you can get pills and energy drinks that can replace a full lunch.

These guarantee the disappearance of the sense of hunger, provide the necessary nutrient supply and are used by those who believe that our bodies do not need food itself, but simply the nutrients it contains. Thanks to 3D printers, you can order and produce such items on site and consume them within seconds. Have fun choosing the taste, size, colour and amount of vitamins, fibres and mineral salts you prefer, or let your devices choose for you.

THE NEW FOOD GIANTS ARE BASED ON THOSE FROM 2020

In 2020, in addition to the multinationals to which we who come from the past are accustomed, a series of technological realities related to food were born, which became the forerunners of the table in 2050. Here are some of them:

- Soylent (meal replacement drink)
- Solazyme (foods produced from algae)
- Hampton Creek (plant products as an alternative to eggs)
- Beyond Meat (in vitro meat)
- NuTek Salt (sodium-free salt)
- Six Foods
- Kite Hill (milk-free cheeses made from seeds and dried fruit)
- Memphis Meat (in vitro meat)
- Impossible Food (vegetable alternatives to meat)
- Finless Foods (in vitro fish)
- Clara Foods (egg proteins)
- Modern Meadow (in vitro meat).

Conservation samples

The refrigerators of the future differ from what a tourist from the present might expect. Many foods can be stored for a long time, thanks to the advances of biotechnology, and others can be kept in special refrigerators that use cryopreservation, maintaining all the characteristics that the food had at the time of freezing.

POISONING IN THE KITCHEN: HACKED ROBOT IN NAPLES

A popular brand of food processor has been used in a very rare case of poisoning. The robot chef, in fact, baked a cake using ammonia for floors instead of ammonia for baking. The cyber police are already on the hunt for motive, and hope to trace the hackers behind the crime.

PRESIDENTS' SCANDAL: ME-EAT CLOSES IN SÃO PAULO

The human meat restaurant chain Me-eat has been forced to close. The Commission has closed the doors of its headquarters in São Paulo, following recent controversy. A few months ago, Me-eat launched a new menu entirely based on the meat of the presidents of the United States of the last hundred years. From analyses carried out in the laboratory, however, the clever marketing move proved to be a clever scam. The meat was obtained from the cells of human beings, but certainly not from those of the presidents.

Sport and leisure time

Sport, music, attractions, cinema and theatre: there are plenty of pastimes available for visitors in 2050, and you'll be spoilt for choice.

If you're looking for fun, jump into at least a couple of the experiences described here. Even if not all its inhabitants agree, accustomed as they are to the infinite possibilities to which they have constant access, for those coming from 2020 and later, there is no doubt: in 2050 it is not possible to get bored.

Sport

Billions of fans around the world, disciplines that combine human and artificial intelligence, new ways to attend events and innovative training techniques make the sport one of the most exciting experiences of 2050.

If you are a sports fan, you need to know one thing right away: spectators do not passively attend sporting events but constantly interact with them. This also applies to all other forms of entertainment, which in 2050 are completely immersive.

If you are a sportsman and would like to keep fit during your visit and practise some sports, you will have many possibilities. Always ask before you start if the equipment is set up for humans, cyborgs or mutants, so as not to risk harming yourself. Medical certificates will not be needed because there will be a check-up immediately before starting.

But first of all, let's take a look at the possibilities that you will have as a "spectator". The use of virtual and augmented reality will allow you not only to take the field with your sporting idols, but to live the experience from the perspective of the athletes themselves.

VIRTUAL REALITY SICKNESS

We recommend that you take special pills that can deceive your brain to avoid the side effects of nausea when using virtual reality. Why should we trick our brains? Simple, when we become immersed in virtual reality our eyes register a movement in space that our body is not perceiving, more or less similar to when we travel by car. In particular, the inner ear does not perceive anything and the brain struggles to record information. The fact is that the brain, which is very protective and also a little paranoid, thinks that the reason of this short circuit is a disease or, worse still, a poison. Nausea is therefore the only solution it has to defend and warn us. In 2050 we understand how to deceive the brain so as not to bypass this annoying side effect of virtual reality so we can enjoy immersive entertainment, courses and culture like never before in history.

Thanks to the new 3D volumetric cameras, it is possible to change points of view, moving between athletes and the crowd in the stands. Football fans will be able to join the goalkeeper of their own team while trying to save a penalty, the attacker during a counterattack or review an action from the referee's point of view, to see if that foul was committed or not. Those who love boxing will feel like they're in the ring, with straight punches, hooks and uppercuts; those who follow basketball will find themselves projected onto the parquet floor, between bats, pick and rolls and wicks; tennis fans will discover what it means to beat a service at Wimbledon. Each action is recorded and analysed and images can be locked and reviewed, skipping from one scene to another.

Athletes also take advantage of augmented reality: within the limits of the rules imposed by each discipline, they can wear devices that provide additional information such as the speed and trajectory of a ball, their heartbeat, the number of patterns available and the remaining time available. This integration between humanity and technology exploits the artificial intelligence that in 2050, by analysing data and statistics, is able to predict what an opponent will do or the tactic with the highest percentage of success. Teams or athletes who have access to more data and more powerful computers therefore have an advantage over their rivals (just as the team with the best athletic trainers has an advantage in the present). They can avoid accidents, optimize performance and anticipate their opponent's moves.

Workouts are all individually customized and precisely adjusted, taking into account health, DNA, predisposition and mood. To complete the picture there are diets and mental preparation, optimized by efficient algorithms. *Neuro-coaching*, for example, can map and rearrange pre-heard information in athletes' brains to increase learning. This technique improves performance so greatly that many have fought to ban it, saying it is a form of brain doping. The argument is similar to those concerning the possibility of wearing intelligent devices and robotic limbs to increase one's physical capabilities. If you want to keep fit and practise some sports during your visit, you can try out some such equipment.

Another controversial aspect of the sport of the future is related to mutant athletes: many parents choose to give birth to a child with a genetic footprint modelled on specific sports, because they dream of a champion in the family. Several adults also decide to modify their own genes to become faster, more resilient or more agile. Thus, in 2050 the athletes are divided into new categories: not only males and females, able-bodied and disabled, but also cyborgs, mutants and humanoids. There are also champions and sports challenges in which humans and machines compete or collaborate with each other, such as a mixed tennis doubles with a human and a cyborg on each team.

Despite these great changes, one thing has remained constant: the ultimate goal of sporting challenges continues to be to arouse emotions and empathy in spectators, as humans, cyborgs or mutants show how they can always exceed their limits.

New sports and stadiums

With the ban on combustion engines, sports related to racing vehicles had to introduce new zero-impact vehicles, completely reinventing themselves. In Formula 1 and Moto GP, all engines are electric (or use other forms of renewable energy) yet can still exceed 370 kilometres per hour. The challenge for car manufacturers is to develop ever more environmentally friendly, technological and efficient motorcycles.

The rules have also changed the places where a sporting challenge can be witnessed: new techno-stages, capable of accommodating over

250,000 people, guarantee spectators an immersive and involving experience. Entering one of these structures, built with carbon-based materials, is like entering a modern temple: a unique and sacred place, sustainable and optimized thanks to sensors and artificial intelligence algorithms. At the entrance to each station, facial-recognition devices and 360-degree cameras identify possible threats, making events and manifestations more secure. The sports show, however, is not the only reason to visit these places, within which dozens of shops, restaurants, cinemas, gyms and virtual simulators guarantee enjoyment even when there are no matches scheduled. Seats on the terraces are automatically assigned by the fan intelligence system implemented in the stands, ensuring people can sit next to friends or those supporting the same team. Each workstation is equipped with an anatomical seat, screens to follow your favourite games up close, and an augmented reality viewer, which provide data, statistics and interesting facts about the players. Holograms and high-definition sound reproducers ensure maximum immersion.

Judges and referees have been replaced by sensors, video cameras and algorithms, and the only humans on the field, in addition to the athletes, are professional entertainers who add spectacle to the event and, with their performances, amaze the spectators. We don't want to lie to you: for those arriving from 2020 the game can be difficult to follow with all these stimuli, but it is worth trying.

In addition to traditional sports, stadiums also host exciting drone-related skill competitions. Divided into two categories (human-guided or robotic), drone-racing is followed all over the world, as are battles between robots in varied disciplines.

FUTURE BOYS 2.0 CHAMPION OF ITALY!

The historic cyborg team, led by Martin, the most advanced robot trainer in Italy, won the soccer championship yesterday. Thanks to his ability to analyse biometric data, DNA and all the historical data of the games played in the past, Martin is able to calculate the best type of training for his players. This is victory not only for the team, but also for the software company, which has established itself as the company providing the best in artificial intelligence.

Immerse yourself in music

Whether you love rock, jazz, rap or classical music, your ears will thank you for taking them into the future. In 2050, music, as with food and medicine, is also functional and can improve your state of health, as well as arousing and enhancing in you particular emotions. To achieve these results, the notes will adapt to your heartbeat, the activity you are doing and, of course, your tastes. If you want to relax or live an experience that takes you into new worlds, you can also use virtual reality and involve all your senses. So get a ticket for at least one concert, because it's worth it.

At the box office you can choose the genre, according to the desired effect on your health and your emotions, the author and the performers. Many options are available: from music composed and performed by humans to music composed by humans but performed by robots, from music written by artificial intelligence algorithms and performed by robots to one of the most exciting shows, where music is composed by algorithms and performed by humans. These are exciting and very special concerts, which merge sparse compositions no musician in the flesh would ever have thought of creating but which, to be interpreted and performed, require extraordinary emotional and empathic skills.

Among the types of concerts available, we would also like to point out those in virtual reality: wherever the artists and their fans are based, they are able to meet in virtual concert halls. The artists not only share concerts or studio sessions via virtual reality, but also a large part of their private lives: fans pay to follow them and see them at work and the proceeds go directly to the musicians, bypassing, in this way, record companies that deal only with advertising and the organization of physical concerts. Music, as with any art form of the future, using systems based on the blockchain, has found new ways to ensure the protection of copyright: now each song is managed directly by the artist, who has control over the all aspects of their music and who is paid for each use.

VIRTUAL COMPOSITION

There are many human composers in 2050 who use technology to aid their music production. Through virtual reality, for example, they can load, wherever they are, one of the "recording studio" scenarios, which will see them in a rehearsal room equipped with piles of musical instruments, together with colleagues from all over the world. Thanks to special gloves they can charge and play all instruments, from guitar to drums, from piano to bagpipes!

Creativity explosions

If you decide to devote time to cultural activities such as film, theatre and exhibitions, it will only take a moment for you to notice the incredible level of attention that is given to creativity, empathy and romantic love. Each event takes place in an atmosphere of great hope, combining pieces of augmented reality, virtual dreams, images and sounds. Collaborations and contrasts of humans, machines and cyborgs create a cultural mix that will leave you breathless, and that are designed to stimulate viewers and turn them into protagonists with an active role within the show itself.

Brain challenges

Online, and in the theatres of 2050, challenges between artificial intelligence and human beings are very fashionable. Quizzes have returned to being one of the most popular forms of entertainment, because they constantly test the skills of algorithms and those of human beings. There are many types of competitions: general culture games, debates, riddles and comic challenges.

NEUROFITNESS

The new technological tools have not caused human beings to lose the desire and the habit of exercising one of their most important organs: the brain. In 2050, great importance was attached to so-called neurofitness: a set of techniques and exercises to train the brain; an essential activity in a world where it is easy to get lazy and rely on technology. The objective of neurofitness is to exploit the neuroplasticity of the brain, i.e. its ability to modify itself on the basis of experience, to sculpt its characteristics and improve its functionalities, just as one does for the body by going to the gym. The most common exercises are meditation, mathematical calculation, languages and philosophical discussions, and these can be done daily or a couple of times a week.

As in the case of sport, there are also various disciplines in neurofitness, including individual or team events. Visit one of the many training centres in the city's districts to get a better idea of this curious new trend.

Astro-tourism

If the sky is not enough for you and your dream has always been to observe the Earth from above, you go on an excursion on the space shuttles for civilian use that allow you to live an authentic experience as an astronaut, complete with custom cabins and partial absence of gravity.

There are numerous and fascinating itineraries available: from a complete tour of our planet to the most famous destinations, such as the Moon or Mars. It all depends on how much time you have available, because the return journey to some destinations may take over two years, depending on the position of the planets at the time of departure.

The Moon, about one third the size of the Earth, is very beautiful to admire from above: approaching its surface in a spaceship is a really exciting experience. For the most passionate, there are tours that allow you to relive the historic moon landing of 20 July 1969 with a walk on the rocky surface. Be careful, however, when you walk: remember that shadows, in the absence of air, are projected in a very different way and without the special viewers that will be supplied you could be deceived into imagining abysses instead of small holes or have to remain totally in the dark for several seconds waiting to get used to the change in brightness in the passage from the sun to the shade.[19] At the lunar space station you can buy souvenirs and shoot souvenir videos in 3D.

For the rest, the Moon is more of a passing hub than a real tourist destination. Many human expeditions only use the Moon as a refuelling station for spaceships: in this way it is easier ships can use fewer resources to leave Earth, and then refuel on the Moon with locally produced fuels.

The real control and sorting centre for what happens on our satellite is not a surface settlement but rather has stations and "warehouses" located in so-called Lagrange points. The particularity of these points is that they manage to create a balance that allows telescopes, materials to be assembled and stations to be parked at a precise point in space, exploiting the forces of attraction of the Earth and the Moon (Figure 19).

Figure 19 The Lagrange points in the Earth–Moon system

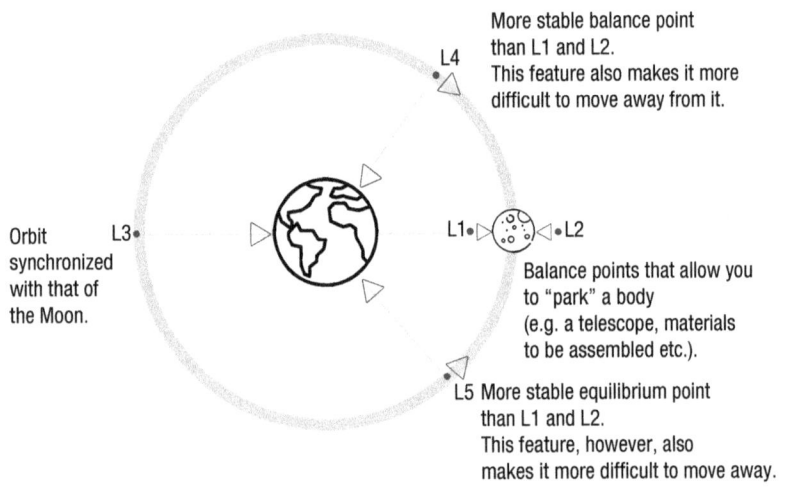

Many expeditions are private and have the purpose of extracting precious metals and minerals from asteroids. This new trend, reminiscent of the historic gold rush, has given rise to many concerns: the inhabitants of 2050 seem to have forgotten the negative effects of colonisations that have marked the history of planet Earth. Public opinion is beginning to demand common rules to manage space conquest with more care and respect, starting with waste disposal.

Among the many routes available, we recommend the trip that goes by the name #dearMoon.[20] After the first tour around the Moon in 2023, which took a group of artists into space, trips have multiplied – partly due to its accessibility: the entire trip takes about a week – and many people have begun to regard this as a once-in-a-lifetime experience.

If you have plenty of time and the length of the journey does not scare you, don't miss a visit to Mars, where you can visit human settlements protected by special biospheric hills with artificial tunnel systems, admire their buildings, built using locally available materials and 3D printers, and read up on ongoing research to make the planet habitable and capable of supporting basic agricultural production. In 2050 the debate on the possibility of artificially creating an atmosphere on Mars is very heated; with an atmosphere, the habitability of the planet would be comparable to that on Earth (Figure 20).[21]

Figure 20 How to create an atmosphere on Mars

MAGNETIC SHIELD	POLE'S BOMBARDMENT	GREENHOUSE GASSES

Creation of a magnetic shield to reduce the effects of the solar wind on the Martian atmosphere (NASA)	Bombing the poles of the planet with electromagnetic pulse bombs to create two suns that would be able to heat the planet. (Elon Musk)	Release gases capable of generating, quickly, the so-called "greenhouse effect" (NASA)

Activation of a heating process allows the release of water reserves, now frozen, and the consequent creation of an atmosphere. The time to achieve an atmosphere like the Earth's, if able to speed up the process of photosynthesis – it is necessary to generate enough oxygen – is at least 200–300 years.

Nature lovers in the northern part of the Red Planet can visit the famous Valles Marineris, the largest expanse of canyons in the Solar System, four kilometres long and with a depth of up to seven kilometres. Flying over this natural paradise is the dream of many inhabitants in 2050, but the cost of travel is still high and is therefore not accessible to all. Not far away, don't miss the Olympus Mons, a huge volcano: the highest in the

Solar System. During the tour, ask the guides, who are humanoid robots, to show you at least one of the impact craters (with meteorites) on the planet: you will be amazed. For the more curious, it is also possible to take a guided tour and fly over the fuel production settlement designed and built by NASA with the aim of exploiting Martian soil to make space missions more efficient. Don't forget to ask to stop and refuel: costs are lower here than on the Moon.

Romantic tours

For the most romantic 2050 offers a holiday on Venus. Technically, however, this is not really a paradise. The most romantically named planet of the Solar System resembles hell much more than paradise: lethal temperatures, close to 460 degrees Celsius, manage to melt lead, even giving rise to "metal rain" in some mountainous areas, the rocky and volcanic landscape is inhospitable, there is a toxic and corrosive atmosphere and oppressive pressure on the surface – all typical characteristics of this destination. Nevertheless, the trip to Venus is unforgettable and highly recommended for those who want to spend time with their soulmate. How is that possible? Simple: the real destination will not be the surface of the planet, but its dense atmosphere, at an altitude of about fifty or sixty kilometres, where, out of the entire Solar System, the pressure and temperature is most similar to the Earth: 20 or 30 degrees Celsius and a pressure similar to that on the top of Kilimanjaro. At this altitude, energy is easily produced due to the proximity of the sun, while the atmosphere is dense enough to protect the tourists from radiation from space.[22]

The classic tour involves staying for about thirty days on an airship on which you are carried by the wind over a bed of clouds, enjoying a floating cruise most loved by couples. The total duration of the outward and return journey is approximately 440 days. If you are madly in love but prefer to limit the time you spend away from the Earth, you can stay for a single weekend on the orbital station (ISS). Although still partly dedicated to scientific and governmental expeditions, the orbital station today caters for tourists. One of the most expensive hotels in the Solar System offers packages lasting from a weekend to a month in an orbital suite: services such as private cabins with large windows for viewing space, equipment for physical exercise and, of course, Wi-Fi. Often, visitors to this hotel opt for the experience of a space walk with a professional.[23]

Who would have thought that a place where it has always been forbidden to sip alcohol or have romantic relationships could become a destination for couples to enjoy aperitifs overlooking the Earth?

For those who like to have their feet on the ground

In case the time available to you is short, or you simply still can't trust the stellar journey, you can remain with your feet on Earth and visit Mars, Venus and the Moon via virtual reality: wearing a special suit you will command humanoid robots to visit destinations that will allow you to explore space without the need to physically go there yourself, yet still be able to interact with the environment as if you were there.

You can also continue to dream of space by witnessing a firework display of shooting stars, which has become very popular since its first appearance in Japan in 2020. The feeling of wonderment is really strong, and even though we know that they are not real shooting stars, seeing dozens of light trails in the sky remains something fascinating for us humans. The display is available on demand and you can book yourself a night of wonder by contacting one of the various companies that offer this type of entertainment.[24]

On Earth, however, one of the most fascinating naturalistic destinations is the Arctic. Due to the warmer climate, areas that were previously inaccessible have opened up to human exploration, revealing totally new and breath taking panoramas. On the other side of the world, the largest natural terrestrial sanctuary, created around 2020 to protect Antarctic fauna and flora from pollution and exploitation by humans, is noteworthy. If you love the sea and you like to dive to discover incredible underwater views, 2050 is not, however, a destination for you. Global warming has badly damaged coral reefs although most of them have been rebuilt using 3D printing technology to preserve their fauna. Special augmented reality shows are often organized for divers to reveal the wonders that only those from the past know from experience our oceans could offer.

Shopping and services

The concept of ownership in 2050 is very different from what we are used to in the present. A blender, an intelligent lawnmower, the bed sheets, the car and a necklace to wear on a romantic evening are seen more as services to rent than as products to own. The watchword in this case is *efficiency*. Only the wealthiest social class enjoys the luxury of purchasing exclusive products that, for the most part, are not used and remain locked up in a drawer or in a box. For most people, however, thanks to the use of artificial intelligence algorithms for the optimization of movement, drones and robots are able to make rapid deliveries of each rented product, thus managing with maximum efficiency the short-term use of the most varied objects.

In any case, shopping in 2050 is an easy and enjoyable activity, even for the lazy. Shops have become real entertainment venues, both virtual and physical, and payments are made so quickly that the risk is not noticing how much one is spending. Scroll through crowded shopping malls, checkout queues, mass publicity campaigns and undifferentiated promotions: the watchwords used to win customers over are emotion, simplicity and customization.

Before you start your shopping tour, remember that items made by humans can be very expensive, much more so than in 2020. To avoid surprises, therefore, always check the prices.

Experiential shops

Be careful, you may not realize you've entered a shop as it appears to be a house, an amusement park or a stadium: in 2050 companies compete to create vibrant, comfortable and original spaces in which people can meet and share experiences and emotions. Buying or renting a product has become synonymous with 360-degree entertainment. The salespeople, both human and robot, have a single task: to arouse positive emotions in customers.

The human staff play an advisory and entertaining role: they act not as simple salespeople, but as sincere and honest friends, able to establish a strong rapport with customers, making the latter feel part of an exclusive and privileged community. Remember, if you choose the service of a human, it is not uncommon for tips to be required. It is best to check at the entrance of the shop so as not to have an unpleasant surprise.

Robot clerks deal with the more technical issues – they will provide you with all the information you need to complete your purchase. These robotic guards, equipped with artificial intelligence and enormous physical strength, connect to the cameras and monitor any suspicious action or movement.

The best shops are open around the clock and offer assistance, information, shows, concerts, film screenings, tastings, massages, courses, parties and other exclusive events for their customers. To improve the experience and optimize the time available, during your stay in the shop you will find only products in line with your expectations and your tastes, while in mildly augmented reality experiences you can try on clothes, hats and much more without having to actually change in the dressing rooms.

To ensure a 100 per cent personalized experience, stores make extensive use of customer biometric data, their DNA and data stored in social profiles. Here too, the considerations made for restaurants and the protection of privacy apply. If you prefer not to allow the use of this data, you should contact the security robots.

SUSTAINABLE BUILDINGS

Like all buildings, commercial buildings also pay great attention to environmental sustainability, which in 2050 is a mandatory condition. To provide a healthy, comfortable and self-sufficient environment, solar panels and electromagnetic induction floors are used. The latter use the customer's steps to create kinetic energy, which in turn is used to power the lights, screens and sound systems in the shops. The air is purified by filters and special absorbent paints that eliminate pollutants such as nitrogen oxides, microbes and bacteria.

Shopping at a distance

Thanks to virtual reality set, in 2050 you can look at and try out clothes, appliances, toys and cars as if they were physically in front of you, without ever having to step into a store. Wherever you are, you can virtually wear a sweater, appreciate the power of a stereo, browse a book or drive a car.

If you want to find out how products are made before you buy them, you can also learn more about them, including, for example, how to make a guitar by visiting a Spanish luthier, or book a tour in any type of factory. For the lazy, there is an automatic personal shopper function: the artificial intelligence device will directly buy what you need, freeing the shopper from the obligation to choose and try out. Finally, the perennially undecided can invite friends, partners or consultants online into their virtual room to show them how a particular pair of boots fits or ask for their opinion on the colour to be chosen for a new bike.

Once selected, the dream article can be delivered anywhere in the world via self-driven trucks, trains and drones, which guarantee very fast delivery times. For some products delivery is guaranteed within ten minutes of ordering. Shopping can also be collected in the shop, so that they can be tested, with the assistance of salespeople.

Tailor-made fashion

In shops, products for sale or rent interact with the external environment: they appear on retractable screens, compose the furnishing of the room, are worn and used by salespeople, are projected in the form of holograms. For prices, promotions and reviews, all you have to do is frame the product that interests you most with your augmented reality face or personal device, switching from physical to digital experience in a fraction of a second. Are you looking for an evening gown? Select with a nod what you prefer: a holographic reproduction as it is or as it will be worn by you.

Almost all products are customizable, especially clothing. If you're looking for a pair of shoes, start by scanning your foot and you can choose the model, the heel height, the material you want to use and then print your shoes using the latest generation of 3D printers.

Intelligent fashion

Just imagine a fabric that can interact with the outside world and integrate touch technologies, such as those of your mobile phone. Imagine that this kind of potential is applied to any item of clothing and any surface, for example those of your furniture. Now, imagine that these fabrics and surfaces lose nothing in terms of comfort, design and practicality. It's not science fiction: all this already exists in 2020 and in 2050 it is normal. The secret is special yarns, able to act as conductors, which, mixed with common materials such as cotton, silk or polyester, can be woven by normal industrial machinery. These are connected to circuits and microscopic sensors that interact with the outside world and that, by connecting to applications and other devices, connect the user to online services and functions. This isn't the end of it. The clothing of 2050 is decidedly different from those to which we are accustomed and uses leathers made from pineapple fibres and animal proteins grown in the laboratory; fabrics made from milk, tea and coffee seeds; fabrics and jeans made with polymers five times thinner than human hair; and special glues that allow clothes to regenerate in case of holes or tears and protect the body from bacteria and infections. All these clothes, as we have seen, interact with the wearer and the surrounding environment: micro-sensors installed in the fabrics monitor and record in real time the body temperature, the calories burned, the heartbeat and the distance travelled. Are you hungry? The sensors will detect it and offer you a snack according to your needs and tastes. These nano-chips also manage to store the energy produced by the body's heat, which can be used to charge any type of device.

Many of the technological applications that affect the world of clothing derive from advances in biotechnology.

Already in 2017 scientists at the Massachusetts Institute of Technology (MIT) were designing clothes that could interact with the environment and change shape based on temperature. Lining Yao, a researcher at the Tangible Media Group, has created an item of clothing that contains living cells that, reacting to body temperature and changes in humidity, guarantee greater ventilation when the body heats up (as happens during sporting activity). Sensors, health checks and much more: everything can now be sewn into clothes and go unnoticed.

SMART CLOTHES

One of the first smart items of clothing was Levi's Commuter Trucker Jacket, a jacket capable of interacting with our devices through the simple touch of a finger. Born from the collaboration between Levi's and the Google Jacquard project, the jacket is one of the flagships of Google ATAP (Advanced Technology and Projects), a special division of Google that develops ideas and programmes to change human life for the better, exploiting technology and new solutions. It is no coincidence that their motto is: "The future is what we choose to make. We make what we believe in. A small band of pirates. Believers. Makers."
In addition to Google, other companies are exploring this world. Francis Bitonti's design studio, among others, has created shoes and clothes made with innovative materials and completely 3D printed, with the stated aim of exploring a new way of imagining fashion.

3D printing hub

Most of the objects around us can be created in 3D. Many people have home printers, but for more complex products there are hubs where you can go and print your product.

CHILD 3D-PRINTS WEAPON AND ACCIDENTALLY INJURES HIS NEIGHBOR'S DOG

Convinced that he had printed out a simple toy, a Canadian child decided to try his new 3D weapon in the garden. A plastic bullet, however, was fired by mistake, injuring the neighbour's dog. "It could have been worse, that's for sure," said the police commander, "but it is necessary to intervene as soon as possible with new laws capable of preventing cases like this."

3D GUNS

In the USA, some models of downloadable guns that could be made using a 3D printer were about to be released for sale on 1 August 2018 by a US company, Defense Distributed, which had previously received approval from the Trump government. In individual states, however, the news was not received positively because of the risk of placing untraceable firearms on the market. A federal judge in Seattle blocked the guns' release a few hours beforehand. That same day the company published on its website a petition (still online at the time of writing) asking that the issue be unblocked and the sale of the models authorized.

The invisible wallet

If you are a distracted person and you often lose your belongings, rejoice: in 2050 you will no longer need your wallet! You can leave it in your suitcase and take advantage of modern devices and services for online payments. With the advent of cryptocurrency and new automated payment systems, physical money has almost completely disappeared, eliminating the need to carry notes, coins or purses. Don't be surprised if you find banknotes used as vintage wallpaper or as design objects.

Even credit cards and national currencies are now little more than a distant memory. This is because payments are made using the new virtual currencies and blockchain technology, and intermediation by banks is pointless and obsolete. Before you leave for 2050, you won't need to open a bank account, withdraw money or change it depending on the country you are visiting. Money will be automatically linked to your account and spendable anywhere. Banks continue to exist, but only carry out financial advisory, investment and credit operations.

With this new approach, money and any other property or contract (the certificate of purchase of a house, a piece of music, an agreement between parties) are kept and owned in the network by the owner, in a completely anonymous form. There is no need to print money, payments are made in real time, without transaction costs, and it is impossible to be cheated or robbed in the traditional sense of the term.

Thanks to the biometric sensors present in all shops, there is no longer any need to queue at the checkout: special detection scanners identify the selected objects and, with a quick retinal-facial examination, add them to the customer's account. Prices change depending on what, when and where we buy: price lists are not fixed, but vary according to facial recognition. Discounts and promotions are personalized and automatically applied, taking into account the time of day and our purchasing habits. All we need to do is take what we need and leave carrying our shopping. In the case of purchases in virtual reality or in places without a scanner, it is possible to pay using any device connected to the network: from the machine to the glasses, all the devices have mounted chips to record data and make payments. The only thing you have to worry about is having enough credit: if you overspend in a shop, you will be invited to return your purchases by kind but inflexible robot guards.

Your hair has value

The year 2050 is a wonderful destination for those who love to style their hair. It is very easy to find private and public hairdressers who offer their services for free in exchange for the data they can collect during the visit. In these specialist beauty salons all services include the opportunity for owners to collect genetic material and to conduct studies on the personality of customers. Special service robots accompany customers throughout their stay in the salon and take note of the casual chatter that is characteristic of these places. If you need a new cut, pay attention to the terms and conditions and be wary of overly favourable offers if you are not willing to take part in such studies.

Seven business deals not to be missed

1. *Bags, shoes and jackets made of human skin.* If you have already read the "Food" section (especially where we have a section on "Animal proteins in vitro", i.e., synthetic meat), you will not be surprised at the possibility of shoes and bags produced from human skin. Initially used for surgical purposes, artificial human skin quickly became a fashionable material and is one of the most sought-after products of 2050.[25] The production process, however, is still long and expensive, which is why human leather accessories are very expensive and are considered luxury goods. If you want something really exclusive, you can also choose to create products from your own skin (in this way we can give someone we love a part of us) or from the skin of famous people, wearing clothes really "signed".
2. *Sustainability diamonds.* The ecological footprint that every tourist or inhabitant leaves on Earth is a very important topic in 2050. The citizens of the future are aware that every activity, movement and consumption of energy has an impact on the environment and measure these indicators with sensors and devices equipped with artificial intelligence. As you wander around the cities, you will notice that there are towers and buildings that absorb pollution and, with the dust they collect, create objects of all kinds. Some of these buildings are equipped with a sensor able to communicate with our devices, calculate the amount of pollution that we have produced and create objects, jewellery and accessories made to measure for us. By purchasing these objects, we can also contribute, economically, to the reduction of our ecological footprint: all revenues are used for programmes to reduce pollution and rebuild ecosystems, as well as to make the pollution absorption system that produces such items work.

3. *Invisibility cloak.* Yes, you read this correctly. Do not think that this is something exclusively related to the future: the first discoveries in this regard date back to the 2010s. Specifically, the invention of invisibility is attributable to the Canadian company HyperStealth, a leader in the camouflage industry. After years of research, the company's scientists have created a material that reads the light around it and generates the illusion of invisibility, deceiving the human senses. This material is called Quantum Stealth and is protected by a host of patents that do not yet allow us to explain its exact operation. In 2050, there are many companies that offer similar products, exploiting plays of light and mirrors that make some objects invisible to our eyes.

4. *Augmented tattoos.* If you are one of those who have never dared to go to a tattoo shop for fear of being able to remove the tattoos, rejoice: in 2050 there are timed, painless and functional tattoos. With these tattoos, you can monitor your physical condition, change the natural characteristics of your skin and much more. Don't take it too lightly, though: in many cases a tattoo is the first step to becoming a cyborg, allowing the fusion of your body with mini-circuits that interact with the outside world.

5. *Lifelong memories.* If, during your trip, you have taken pictures, shot videos or produced 3D models, or if you have other digital memories to take with you, don't worry: in 2050 there are many systems that allow you to store huge amounts of data in a small space. Among the various models available, the DNA card from 150 petabytes (150 million gigabytes) is very small, very light (it weighs less than a gram) and is also injectable under the skin. It costs little and will allow you to have enough space, with a guaranteed duration of a million years.

6. *Living lamps.* Our house will have a whole different atmosphere with the light of a bacterial lamp. These are made from bacteria that have been genetically modified to light up in the dark and are inserted into designer containers.

7. *Spider scarves.* The possibility of producing all types of furs in the laboratory has sparked the imagination of many fashion houses. One of the most weird and expensive products of 2050 is the spider skin scarf, very soft to the touch, light and very, very, very fashionable.

Children

Each city from 2050 is equipped to accommodate families. Parents will find everything they need for the care of even the youngest child, and can also rely on the indispensable help of robotic babysitters. These automatons, equipped with artificial intelligence, are programmed to interact with children and both educate and entertain them.

There is no shortage of attractions and theme parks, or of museums (where admission is free for all youngsters) that offer rooms and exhibitions dedicated to all ages.

If you are interested in virtual reality, remember that this is forbidden to children under 16 years of age as it can cause pathological dependence and, for this reason, is reserved for adults.

Health

Travel and health

Scientists and researchers have known this for years: travelling is good for your health. Exploring new places and experiencing other cultures stimulates creativity, cognitive flexibility and depth of thought, with beneficial effects on both body and mind. People who travel are happier, healthier and psychologically stronger. But travelling in 2050 also has other hidden benefits (reserved, however, for those who are relatively well off): taking advantage of the advances of medicine you can improve your health, relying on artificial intelligence, microscopic sensors, nanotechnologies, 3D printers, robotics, biotechnology, big data, genomics, use of stem cells and all the technologies that have revolutionized the medicine of the future. Many time travellers choose 2050 precisely for this reason: to have access to treatments that do not exist in the past.

QUARANTINE

Like all buildings, commercial buildings also pay great attention to health. If you are visiting 2050 for the first time, don't be frightened by the signs indicating that travellers from the past must be quarantined: it lasts for just under forty minutes. You will be asked to enter a special room where silent diagnostic robots will per-

form a total screening of your body and eliminate the germs, viruses and bacteria that have accompanied you from the present, diagnosing any diseases, suggesting treatments and prevention and preventing the proliferation of diseases eradicated for decades.
IMPORTANT: To prevent your body from succumbing to new diseases that do not exist in 2020, you will be required, for your own safety, to undergo some compulsory vaccines. Anyone who refuses to be vaccinated will be obliged to return to the present.

Sensors and microscopes everywhere

Diagnosing probable diseases in advance is one of the best ways to combat and prevent them. In 2050 we are witnessing an exponential application of this concept, with enormous benefits both in terms of well-being and in terms of public spending on medical care for patients. There are plenty of ways to constantly monitor your health. Among the most widespread we can mention:

- *Augmented mirrors*: these special devices, which can be found in city homes and offices, use the analysis of images, videos and scans in 3D to calculate in real time any cardio-metabolic risks, the state of sight and that of the skin.
- *Portable devices*: these are equipped with lenses that turn them into real microscopes, for very fast and inexpensive tests, so that you always have a digital diagnostic laboratory in your pocket.
- *Functional garments*: many garments are equipped with minute sensors that monitor heartbeat, breathing and sweating.
- *Ingestible technologies*: among the things you would never dream of ingesting is certainly an electronic stethoscope. But what if it's small enough to fit in a pill? In 2050, it is common to make use of tiny tracking systems, built with nanotechnologies and ingestible orally, that can improve heart rate, breathing and body temperature, sending the data to the connected devices or, in the most serious cases, directly to health centres, so that medical professionals can intervene in time.
- *Biometric tattoos*: made with a particular conductive ink (i.e. capable of transmitting energy), these temporary tattoos are connected to specific devices and transfer, measure and record the position of a person and their body values.

HEALTH MIRROR

It is called Wize Mirror and it is a project developed thanks to European funds and coordinated by Sara Colantonio, an Italian researcher at the CNR of Pisa. Just look at yourself in this special technological object to get some real-time advice on your health.[26]

Databases

In 2050 everyone (including travellers, after the initial quarantine) are listed in central databases. These databases may be more or less confidential under the relevant legislation. In some cases, DNA and recorded data are automatically made available to research centres and doctors: the more data available, the more algorithms learn to identify diseases, resulting in improved health, although there are still issues of privacy and data security to be overcome. Some insurance companies and employers, for example, apply discriminatory policies towards individuals predisposed to certain diseases. Many countries have discussed welfare policies and selective schooling, preferring to invest in those who are more likely to live a long and healthy life, rather than in people with a predisposition to serious diseases.

For this reason, we will never stop recommending that you always carefully check the privacy rules applied in the places you visit, so as not to find yourself robbed of the most precious code you have: your DNA.

Digital hospitals

More than just hospitals, in 2050 these are mobile structures that can be made available to patients wherever they are. Hospitals have undergone a process of digitization and decentralization, achieved by exploiting the innovations introduced by immersive telemedicine, virtual surgery and portable instrumentation. For the most vulnerable, it is easy to come across compact medical areas, which, if necessary, become operational hubs, where emergency drones can deliver instruments and medicines. These areas are also equipped to perform surgical operations, thanks to the applications of robotics and virtual reality (see the section "Doc Bot"). Doctors can operate and check up on patients remotely, while for a diagnosis you can request the certified consultation of hundreds of experts, through platforms that use blockchain technology.

BIOBANKS

In 2009, Ezekiel Emanuel, a consultant to US President Barack Obama, declared that, according to his view, citizens should be obliged to participate in clinical research, allowing all doctors access to their data, including those about DNA. The reasoning starts from the assumption that, with more data available, studies on diseases and their correlations become more effective. Consequently, according to Emanuel, citizens would be morally obliged to donate their data, renouncing individual freedom in favor of a Common Good.
Iceland also had a similar approach in 1998, when it launched the deCode Genetics project, with the aim of mapping the genetic code of all its citizens. The project, however, failed within a short time, due to pressure from those who claimed their right not to take the test.

Customized for the individual

Big data, artificial intelligence, genomics and biology have revolutionized the world of medicine and allow doctors to treat each patient in a personalized way. For this reason, when the inhabitants of 2050 think of the past, they find it hard to understand that different people can be treated in the same way. Nonetheless, not all future patients can afford personalized treatments and medicines so some end up adopting generic methods that are now considered outdated.

Code issue

All diseases have a genetic foundation and, thanks to DNA mapping, scientists can read and understand many of the correlations between genes and disease development. There is a lot of information contained in DNA: from one's probable physical appearance to a predisposition to get sick, from one's ability to lose weight to main behavioural traits. Starting from this foundation, in 2050 those who have the means can use genetic engineering to correct any errors in their DNA.

DNA TEST

Today there are several services that allow you to sequence your DNA. One of the most accessible (at the time of writing of this book the cost is €99) is the one offered by 23andMe, which, starting from a sample of saliva, provides a complete file of codes that represent the genes in the DNA of a person. On the 23andMe European website (https://www.23andme.com/en-eu/) you can use the data to find distant relatives and discover the geographical origin of your ancestors. But the data can also be used in other online services, which can give us a general idea of the predispositions to diseases statistically associated with our genes. For those who want a complete analysis, including medical advice, the price is a few thousand euros.

Attention! 23andme has a low cost because it also functions as a DNA bank and stores all data for analysis and study purposes, so be careful to check the small print. Before undertaking the test you can ask not to be registered and no record kept of your DNA.

Because of the enormous value of these data, several companies are trying to establish themselves as reference points for the sector. An example is Helix (https://www.helix.com/): an online platform through which you can manage personalized diets, fitness tips, medical prevention and other programmes based on your DNA.

The medicines of the future are also specifically designed to be more effective and act in a targeted manner according to the composition of the patient's DNA. Different people respond differently to different medicines and pharmacies, which have become automatic distributors scattered throughout cities, use 3D printers and artificial intelligence to create the perfect remedy for each individual.

For diseases that require special interventions, there are, finally, the nanobots: robots in "nano" format, the result of studies of nanotechnology, which can be injected or ingested. These mini-robotic doctors are able to move very easily within the body and "deliver" medicines to the right cells with extraordinary precision.

HOW SMALL IS "NANO"?

The applications of nanotechnology are many and promise to revive sectors such as information technology, medicine, transport, food, the environment and many others. The advantages of nanotechnology lie in the possibility of creating and producing microscopic devices (smaller than one nanometre, i.e., one billionth of a metre).
To give you an idea of the measures we are talking about:

- the double helix of DNA measures about 2/2.5 nanometres
- our nails grow at a rate of one nanometre per second
- a sheet of paper is about a hundred thousand nanometres thick
- a bacterium is a thousand nanometres long.

Now that we have clarified the order of magnitude, we can try to figure out what incredible applications a technology capable of operating on this scale can bring, opening our imagination to a world of almost infinite possibilities. By intervening at this level on materials, it is possible to improve and enhance some of their essential qualities, creating products that are more durable, stronger, lighter, more reactive, better conductors and much more, depending on their use and desired effects.

Printed organs, tissues and other biological materials

One of the (undesirable) effects of the reduction in extra-violent accidents is the proportional reduction in the number of organs donated by the victims. In 2050, however, giant strides were made in the 3D printing of biological materials, and some organs, the epidermis and blood can be produced synthetically in the laboratory, where their characteristics are designed and customized as needed, thus avoiding, among other things, the risk of potential rejection by the recipient. The costs of this technology are still high, but are decreasing, and it is hoped that soon synthetic organs will be accessible to the majority of the population.

Doc Bot

Lasers, micro-robots, neural interfaces and precision instruments allow physicians to complete or programme interventions designed to reduce the number of invasive wounds, recovery times, costs and, last but not least, the patient's pain. All this can also be done remotely, thanks to virtual reality and telemedicine, which make it possible to operate remotely in a simple and reliable manner, eliminating travel problems and allowing for much more flexible management of emergencies. The robots are programmed to perform highly complex operations, transplants, organ removals, but also aesthetic touch-ups and beauty interventions. The machines also provide doctors with the ability to reduce errors and allow manoeuvres that are impossible for human hands, with levels of precision unattainable to the naked eye.

INTELLIGENT ULTRASOUND: IT'S CONTROVERSIAL

The intelligent ultrasound Marcus is on trial: it failed to recognize the signs of a rare disease, thus causing the death of one patient. Marcus Inc., the company behind Marcus algorithm, defends itself by claiming they have no responsibility on data contained in the Marcus database; the doctors think otherwise, and claim that it is a bug in the system. The relatives of the victim demand an answer: who is going to be held responsible?

Overcoming disabilities

In 2050, exoskeletons, nurse robots, interfaces, chips and circuits merge with human beings and allow people with disabilities to live a freer and more independent life. The neural- control interface, also known as the brain–computer interface,[27] connect exoskeletons and artificial limbs and allow people with motor disabilities or older people to (re)gain mobility and control the movement of robotic hands and arms.

Even those suffering from chronic pain live with greater serenity, as their suffering can be relieved thanks to special interfaces implanted in the cerebral cortex.

The blind, through a robotic retina (a sort of video camera that communicates with the brain by stimulating neurons), obtain significant improvements in vision, while the deaf use microscopic devices that help to perceive and interpret sounds from the outside environment as a means of communication.

Memory

If you have memory problems or simply want to increase your intellectual capacity, you can do so by using electrical stimuli or one of the increasingly popular cerebral foam implants that can be inserted into the cranial vault.

New diseases

One of the biggest medical challenges of 2050 is infections: due to the genetic evolution of bacteria, which have become ultra-resistant to antibiotics, the drugs used in the past no longer work. Much hopes is placed in the development of nanotechnologies: creating ad hoc nano-antibiotics that can eliminate even the most resistant bacteria.

Another field exposed to new problems is that of psychology, which in 2050 also includes cybersecurity: most cyborgs are in fact equipped with brain implants that, if hacked, can cause pain and, to a lesser degree, new, frightening diseases; some cyborgs, moreover, struggle to accept the new reality in which they have been immersed since having their implants.

Among other psychological dysfunctions, the most widespread are virtual reality obsession, with millions of people spending almost all of their time in the virtual world, and struggling to return to the real world, and robophobia, which consists of a feeling of hatred towards robots, caused by the fear that machines will steal jobs and/or partners, and replace human beings.

Many have developed a real addiction to known drugs, which can create imbalances comparable to addiction to alcohol, smoking and drugs.[28] Others suffer from imbalances due to the development of obsessions with tracking themselves: they cannot resist the temptation to collect data and analyse any activity carried out, as well as their vital parameters, even when these are absolutely perfect, sometimes putting at risk their security and privacy in order not to lose any useful data.

Moreover, more and more people are suffering from technological isolation disorders (which Sherry Turkle of MIT in 2017 called "Alone together", "to be alone together"[29]) and therefore resort to the support of a psychologist.

Other psychophysical diseases include cybernetic septicaemia, caused by unexpected reactions to cybernetic implants to the detriment of the body and the mind; nanotoxicological shocks, caused by unwanted nanoparticles and nanomaterials in the environment; psychosis induced by advanced intelligence: excessive brain potential can create imbalances in the human nervous system, with consequent attacks of anxiety, high degrees of mania and anti-social behaviour.

Never die

Death is a technical problem, a disease, and there are those who believe that, like all diseases, we can prevent and avoid it. That's why in 2050 researchers are working to push the life expectancy of human beings beyond 400 years, with the goal of achieving amortality.

The treatments that use stem cells to slow down the aging process of the brain are also moving in the same direction. Bill Maris, founder of Google Venture, is famous for this sentence: "I just hope to live long enough not to die."[30]

Being amortal means not getting sick and not getting old, but it does not exclude death altogether: in the event of an accident death is always possible.

The desire for immortality is hard to kill: many individuals decide to digitally track their entire lives, their thoughts and their interactions, and then download them to hardware and artificial intelligence software, thus becoming, in the broadest sense, immortal. Not everyone regards this as a real way of prolonging their lives. There are still too many doubts about what can happen to a mind that, disconnected from a biological body, interacts with the outside world without the five senses. This attempt at immortality is not without its risks of hacking and poses enormous problems of liability and damage: switching off hardware or deleting data could be tantamount to murder.

SIDE EFFECTS OF IMMORTALITY

No matter what way you try to reach them, amortality and immortality are not only scientific and mathematical challenges, but also psychological and social ones. This is a goal that could have profound effects on the individual, as well as on society as a whole. It only takes a little imagination to imagine how, with a potentially eternal life, the meaning of marriages, studies, works and institutions would change profoundly, as would reproduction, which could turn from a positive event into a problem. Going even further, we can think of possible psychosis and reactions of those who, in order not to risk dying in, for example, a traffic accident, decide to "live" eternally in a protective capsule, reducing their experiences to virtual ones. The concept of suicide would be distorted: taking one's own life could become a normal thing, an act necessary to make room for new human beings or to escape from the boredom of a millenary life.

This scenario could lead to the proliferation of ad hoc services for suicides: from offers for the best possible death, to the realization of one's last will and testament, to the complete organization, in advance, of one's own funeral.

Transportation

There are so many activities you can do and so many new things to see in 2050 that the time available may seem like it's never enough. The good news, however, is that travel is not a problem and you can get around the planet in the blink of an eye. Not to mention that travelling via future means is often, in itself, an extraordinary experience.

Moving around the city

Did you leave your driver's licence on the bedside table before you left? Don't worry: in 2050 your driver's licence is just a distant memory. Whether you choose to travel by car, plane, train or Hyperloop, during your trip you can move around without ever needing to drive (unless you decide to do so because driving is your passion or as a new form of entertainment).

Self-driving cars have replaced most human-driven vehicles, significantly reducing the number of road accidents due to distractions, excessive driving, falling asleep, drink-driving, disregarding safety distances, substandard tyres, improper manoeuvres or mobile phone use. To understand how important this innovation is, it is enough to consider that in the present accidents caused by the reasons listed cause about 1.3 million deaths every year, representing the leading cause of death for individuals between 15 and 29 years.[31] In the United States, 94 per cent of these accidents are due to human error,[32] while in Italy the estimate is around 41 per cent.[33]

In 2050, it is not only lives (millions) that are saved by this new means of transport, but also time. Thanks to more efficient vehicles and the resulting reduction in traffic, the time saved is estimated to exceed 250 million hours per year. If we then take into account that the time devoted to driving can be exploited to the full, these hours multiply disproportionately.[34] The on-board computers take care of everything themselves: connecting to the network, they collect data from other cars to monitor traffic and decide on the fastest route, suggesting the best time to leave and helping passengers to optimize their time. The information recorded interacts online with the myriad of data collected by the public administration software that measures and monitors all urban activities. A constant dialogue is developed between vehicles and all types of network infrastructure: energy, transport, buildings and public activities exchange data with each other in order to set priorities, optimize resources and make the lives and movements of citizens simpler and more comfortable. In order to maintain individual safety standards, each car only starts when the passengers have their seatbelts fastened; in addition, accurate relocation sensors ensure that in the event of obstacles or unforeseen events, the vehicle automatically brakes. The interior of the car is designed to facilitate a wide variety of passenger activities, so people can take advantage of the space available and devote the time of the journey to working, reading, studying, singing, sleeping, eating, applying make-up with a real mirror (not with the rear-view mirror), playing, partying, listening to music, having a massage (strictly by robots) and much more. Before choosing the vehicle that suits you, therefore, assess the interiors, the services included and read the reviews of other users carefully.

Some companies offer free trips in their cars. Be careful, however: as with restaurants, often the price to be paid is the transfer for commercial purposes of all your data, including biometric data. Therefore, carefully check the terms and conditions of use before accepting. If you want to save money without relinquishing your privacy, you can use public transport. Autonomous, but less personalized than a private service, it is optimized to follow the routes of the majority of passengers and make stops calculated according to the position of those to be picked up and the destinations of those already on board.

A new urbanism

Travelling through the streets of 2050 we can see numerous changes dictated by the need to adapt urban planning to new means of transport.

In the spaces dedicated to self-driving vehicles, digital information networks have supplanted traffic lights, signs, licence plates, fire brigades, speed cameras and policemen. Everything is digital and embedded in algorithms and is shown on augmented reality systems only when there is a need to interact with a human being (something that happens very rarely).

There are no more parking spaces: except for a few luxury brands dedicated to a very small niche of customers, cars are no longer the property of individuals, but belong to companies that offer them as a service and optimize their movements by keeping them constantly in use.

Cleaner engines

In 2050 it is forbidden to use engines that run on fossil fuels such as oil. In their place there are several other "clean" alternatives. The most common are electric motors, which thanks to special asphalts, hybrid engines and those that use biofuels, are recharged while on the go.

Self-driving cars: Dedicated lanes

The first model of self-driven vehicle dates back to 1974, but the first to become truly famous was the Google Car, in 2009.

In the past, this type of vehicle, which in 2050 is now in common use, was the subject of much discussion, both because of its urban and social impacts and because of the doubts raised in public opinion, which for years has been divided over its use. A 2015 study by the Boston Consulting Group showed that nearly half of the respondents preferred cars built by traditional manufacturers rather than by companies like Apple or Google. Sixty-five per cent of respondents said they did not want their children to be in these vehicles. In 2050 things have changed, even though these issues still give rise to great controversy with regard to the possibility of programming artificial intelligence systems to take decisions potentially capable of putting the life of a human being at risk. MIT has created an online test, called the Moral Machine, which allows users to simulate possible danger situations and indicate the choice that the car should make. While, despite great cultural differences,[35] all users appear rational in their computer responses and choose to "save" as many lives as possible, almost no one is willing to relinquish their own life, even if this means saving ten others.[36]

How, then, was it possible to overcome the obstacle of trust and to make self-driving vehicles so widespread in 2050? The secret is the context: self-driving cars have special dedicated lanes. Instead of programming the means to take decisions related to typical situations of danger to that which arise when a human is driving (that is, drivers becoming distracted, a sudden obstacle in the middle of the road or the abnormal behaviour of another driver), it was decided to isolate this car and use them only on dedicated lanes.

In this way self-driving cars do not endanger human lives and avoid finding being placed in situations where, despite technological progress, artificial intelligence cannot really be programmed like a human brain.

Artificial morality

Moral choices made by humans have been very well studied and are still widely discussed. What we can observe is that all learning software, when compared to a human being, has a distinctive characteristic: it inevitably displays excessive zeal, because it is not programmed to break, from time to time, some rules, with the help of that "magic" ingredient called common sense. Figure 21 explains why the absence of common sense in artificial intelligence systems is a problem.

Figure 21 Driving school: Continuous and dashed lines

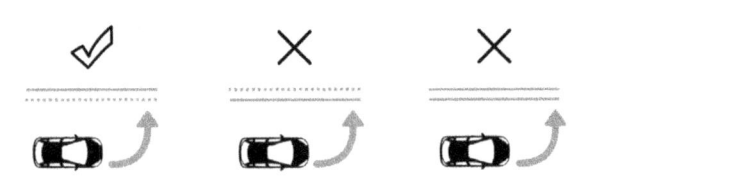

Let's take an example: let's assume that the software is programmed to slavishly follow the rules of the override code and that, at the same time, an emergency occurs that requires a car to drive to the nearest hospital as soon as possible. One of the rules of the code is that you may not overtake by crossing a continuous line on the road, but you may do so if the line is dashed. The leftmost car in Figure 21 can therefore overtake as the nearest line to it is dashed; the car in the middle and the one on the right cannot as the line next to them is continuous. So what happens to a self-driving car in an emergency situation where a human being would use common sense and decide to break the rules? The car does not change its behaviour and, without exception, continues to follow the rules.

As shown in Figure 22, it is very easy to deceive a self-driving car. It would be enough to draw two circles, one continuos and one discontinuous (as represented in Figure 22). In this case, the car would drive straight into the circle and, as if it was a black hole, would never be able to get out. A human driver, on the other hand, would probably evaluate the situation carefully and then decide to escape the trap, using common sense, crossing the continuous line and continuing their journey, without being considered guilty of having violated the rules of the road. The truth is that situations like these happen every day, more often than you realize, and we humans have the extraordinary ability to make common-sense decisions based on the context in which we find ourselves.[37]

Figure 22 Autonomous car traps

Source: Schematic reworking of the logic underlying the work of J. Bridle, *Autonomous Trap 001*, 2017.

This is what happens when we avoid an obstacle by invading the opposite lane (if there is no danger in doing so); when we decide to hide information from someone because we know that it is not important and could hurt them; when we convince a hostess on a low-cost flight to let us take an extra handbag on the plane, showing that there would still be room to keep it in the one suitcase allowed; or, finally, when we take a woman in labour to hospital and break any rule of the road to get her there as soon as possible.

Right? Wrong?

The truth is that we don't really know which it is, and there is no single answer on which everyone agrees. Since childhood, we have been taught that there are rules, absolute laws that always apply without exception, and guidelines that help us to make decisions but that must be contextualized using common sense, evaluating rewards and benefits and learning to predict the small and large impacts that their violation may involve. So society works also thanks to small lies, small contraversions and a lot of common sense. Excessive zeal, on the other hand, is often a degeneration of the establishment of the law.

When we try to teach an algorithm the rules of morality we are doomed to fail, because we cannot specify the abstract concept of common sense that is based on a number of cultural factors and is subjective and experiential. Even in 2050, humans are still unable to decipher this, let alone teach it to software. At most, and this is what has been done in 2050, it is possible to feed artificial intelligence so much historical data, in patterns, examples and choices made over time, to allow it to imitate, with a good approximation, the decisional mechanism of a human being.

We stress: *imitate*. This does not mean that the algorithm consciously understands what it is doing, but that it is so good at imitating us that it manages to deceive even us, making us believe that it has reasoned like a real person because it makes the same choice that we would have made, even if it follows a different mechanism. This is a process that, if you think about it, resembles the one by which children learn: observation, experience, repetition and imitation are the key to learning behaviours, rules, moral guidelines and much more.

Shared mobility

The urban centres of 2050 are a paradise for shared mobility. Bicycles built with special materials that do not rust, electric scooters, hoverboards, cars of all shapes and sizes: all vehicles are shared and localized through apps. Find out which are near you and choose the vehicle that best suits your needs – you will not be disappointed.

Hyperloops, trains and other vehicles

The ideal way to move around for those who need to travel long distances quickly is undoubtedly the Hyperloop: a means of underground transport that allows you to travel at over 1,200 kilometres per hour. It is a sort of convoy, composed by pressurized capsules "leaning" on an air cushion running inside a tube kept at low pressure in order to reduce the friction. Hyperloop allows passengers to travel faster than by plane, spending less than a normal train and with a resounding energy saving. For example, it only takes twenty-five minutes to get from Milan to Rome.

If Hyperloop networks now connect almost all the capitals of the planet, trains continue to be used for regional journeys or for the transport of goods: do not picture, however, the old wagons that run on rails to which we are accustomed in the present. Thanks to the laws of magnetism, which are part of quantum physics, engineers have been able to successfully create vehicles that travel using magnetic levitation, without touching the rails, and are able to exceed speeds of more than 600 kilometres per hour.

LEVITATION AND HYPERLOOP

If you've been to Shanghai in the late 2010s, you probably have already been on a vehicle that uses the magnetic levitation technology: the MagLev, which connects the city with its airport.
As for Hyperloop, its development – at least as a project – dates back to the early 2010s. While California was going to invest $69 billion in a plan to create a very high-speed rail link between Los Angeles and San Francisco, Elon Musk – the founder of Tesla, SpaceX and other companies that had a strong impact on 2050 – published a program in which he claimed he could do the same thing by spending a tenth of that sum. All thanks to the new means of transportation that Musk had thought of, which was destined to bring a revolution to the future way of transportation: the Hyperloop. The project gained immediate attention and has since evolved enormously. In 2050, Hyperloop has become a widespread standard and it holds the best combination of the three most determinant parameters: cost, capacity, and speed.

Magnetic levitation is also used to move other vehicles, the most famous of which are undoubtedly hoverboards, authentic semi-flying skateboards used for small and short trips and loved in particular by young people.

The "sky is (not) the limit": in the future, you just have to look up to see an incredible array of planes and flying machines. Flying cars can take off and land vertically like helicopters, without the need for large landing areas and are small enough to move smoothly between buildings and skyscrapers. Even more amazing, we realize that the airways are crowded with individuals speeding through the sky like bird men. Equipped with special electrically propelled backpacks, the most famous of which is the Jetpack, many inhabitants of 2050 fly from one part of the city to the other every day using this method.

Many aircraft are self-piloted, like cars, and are used for passenger transport and the delivery of food and other goods.[38] In the case of particularly long journeys, civil planes remain an option to be taken into consideration: using ground-borne flight they can connect two places at the antipodes, such as London and Sydney, in just two and a half hours. The external structure of the planes, which resemble the shape of a bird more than a means of transport, is composed of a membrane of biopolymers able to control the light, humidity and temperature inside, while numerous areas within the plane dedicated to leisure and suitable for all types of passengers help to make the trip more enjoyable. Don't be frightened if the airplane changes shape on the way: these modern structures are built to adapt to weather conditions.

If you are particularly sensitive to environmental issues, you will be happy to know that, at least in part, 2050 aircraft are powered by electricity generated by special solar panels. Research is trying to find a way to ensure that they are able to run completely on this clean energy source; the results, however, are not satisfactory so far and we will have to wait a little longer.

Forget queues and controls, taking a plane has become much faster and easier in 2050. Automatic checks with facial recognition, luggage transported directly from home to your destination and airports built as entertainment centres have completely changed the travel experience.

Spacecraft

For a traveller from 2020, simply getting on one of the civilian spacecrafts in operation in 2050 is already an incredible experience. If you've been waiting a lifetime to do this, get a round-trip ticket to the new orbital station right away: it'll cost less than trips organized by space agencies, and you'll still be able to admire the curvature of the Earth.

ORIGINS OF DRONES

A drone is an airborne vehicle that can be manoeuvred remotely or completely automatically. The commercial success of the drones is linked to their ability to travel for several kilometres and to use four-propeller stabilization to remain stationary at a precise point while in the air. As with many technological innovations, drones derive from war research and were used for the first time during the First World War, when they served different purposes, from bombing to aerial reconnaissance of strategic areas.
In 2050, drones are the most widely used means of delivering products, medications and medical devices (such as defibrillators, in an emergency).

Dreaming of teleportation

Travelling, moving, sending and receiving objects: in 2050 they are all easy and fast actions. There is an invention, however, which, for over a hundred years, has aroused the interest of scientists, physicists and engineers and allows the time spent to move people and things to decrease to zero: teleportation. Unfortunately, in 2050, teleportation has not yet been achieved, but it remains a very interesting and studied topic.

Even today, a team of physicists seems to have found an algorithm capable of secretly transmitting information from one place to another, using quantum cryptography.[39] In fact, this group may have identified a system of recreating in a distant place a sort of copy of the original: a physical reproduction of an object or person. In practice, this is not a "real" teleport as we have imagined it up to now, but something more like ubiquity.

This research has become the basis for a new area of teleportation science, which attracts a great deal of attention in 2050. In the meantime, even in 2050, inhabitants have to remain satisfied with 3D printing and sending models over the airwaves that can be printed and then rematerialized anywhere on the planet or in space.

TELEPORTATION

Until 2013, someone in Google had the title of Head of Teleportation printed on their business cards. This was not a joke. It was in fact a Google project that was cancelled and abandoned in 2013, after the group that was working on it came to the conclusion that to materialize an object in a distant place it was necessary to destroy it first, which would have blocked the door to possible practical applications.

Notes

[1] L.C. Smith, *The World in 2050*, New York, Dutton Books, 2010.
[2] F. Franzosi *et al.*, "An innovative approach to the assessment of hydro-political risk: a spatially explicit, data driven indicator of hydro-political issues", *Science Direct, Global Environmental Change*, 52 (2018), 286–313.
[3] Genetic recombination was invented by Stanley Cohen and Paul Berg of Stanford University and Herbert Boyer of the University of California in San Francisco.
[4] For example, the project "The Great Passenger Pigeon Comeback", has been recreating the passenger pigeon, extinct in 1914.
[5] C. Parmesan, G. Yohe, "A globally coherent fingerprint of climate change impacts across natural systems", *Nature*, 421 (6918), January 2003, 37–42.
[6] T.L. Root *et al.*, "Fingerprints of Global Warming on Wild Animals and Plants", *Nature*, 421 (6918), January 2003, 57–60.
[7] The so-called cave bear was first discovered in 2006 in the Canadian Arctic. Polar bears travel to the southern islands as a result of polar warming, thus it is possible to create these hybrids between species with similar DNA but adapted to different natural habitats.
[8] If we think that the price of a meat hamburger produced in vitro has fallen from about 330,000 dollars in 2013 to about 11 dollars in 2018, it is easy to see how in 2050 it is a valid and affordable alternative to meat produced in the traditional way.
[9] TED is the trademark of a conference company founded in 1984 in Silicon Valley and then developed globally under the TEDx brand.

[10] Nicholas Negroponte (b. 1943) is a US scientist famous for his innovative studies in the field of the interfaces between man and computer.
[11] "My prediction is that we will ingest the information. You're going to swallow one and you'll know English, swallow a pill and you'll know Shakespeare a- king..."
[12] See item D.B. Grigg, "Rivoluzioni agricole", in *Enciclopedia delle scienze sociali*, treccani.it.
[13] S. Roversi, "Future food for climate change: le grandi sfide del food tech", *Nòva*, 7 June 2018.
[14] Being a cannibal in 2050 is not always considered a crime as it is possible to create any type of meat in the laboratory without harming in any way the animal – including man – from which it is produced.
[15] C. Lippert, R. Sabatini *et al.*, "Identification of individuals by trait prediction using whole-genome sequencing data", PNAS, 114 (38), September 2017, 19.
[16] To produce one kilogram of beef, about 15,000 litres of water are needed, compared with 287 litres needed to produce one kilogram of potatoes. Institution of Mechanical Engineers, "Global food: Waste not, want not", imeche.org, 2 November 2013.
[17] Proteins created in the laboratory are called synthetic or in vitro proteins to indicate how they were obtained.
[18] A. Van Huis, J. Van Itterbeeck *et al.*, *Edible Insects: Future Prospects for Food and Feed Security*, Rome, FAO, 2013.
[19] On Earth, the light that casts a shadow comes from the sky. The molecules in the terrestrial atmosphere diffuse sunlight (blue more than red) in all directions, and part of that light lands in the shadows. That's why the footprints we leave on sunlit snow are blue. On the Moon, however, the shadow is dark and receives no light from the sky as there is an absence of air.
[20] The #dearMoon project, which plans a trip around the Moon in 2023, was announced by Elon Musk in 2018. Aboard the Falcon Heavy rocket will be Japanese entrepreneur Yusaku Maezawa and a group of artists selected from among the best on our planet.
[21] The discussion is heated and proceeds in the form of academic articles and Tweets. For a taste, see B. Gallagher, "So can we terraform Mars or not?", *Nautilus*, 11 October 2018.
[22] HAVOC (High Altitude Venus Operational Concept) is a project concerning a mission to Venus, currently being studied by NASA. See "HAVOC: High Altitude Venus Operational Concept: An Exploration Strategy for Venus", NASA Technical Report, available online on the NASA Technical Report Server.
[23] K. Korosec, "Russia is planning to build a luxury hotel on the International Space Station", *Fortune*, 28 December 2017.
[24] The Japanese start-up ALE Co. (Astro Live Experiences, http://star-ale.com/en/) aims to send two small satellites into orbit. These will cause a rain of specially designed particles to fall to Earth, which, when they come into contact with the atmosphere, will catch fire and thus mirror the characteristic wake of shooting stars.
[25] In 2016, a student named Tina Gorjanc, launched the Pure Human project: creating a line of products made with human skin recreated in the laboratory from the DNA of Alexander McQueen, with the aim of highlighting the legislative

vacuum that allowed this to be done. For further information, please visit Tina's website: http://dropr.com/tina_gorjanc.

[26] For more information, see "Wize Mirror: uno specchio per mantenersi sani", 31 July 2015, https://www.cnr.it/it.

[27] A neural interface is a tool that allows direct communication between the brain and an external medium (usually a computer).

[28] E. Peper, R. Harvey, "Digital addiction: increased loneliness, anxiety, and depression", neuroregulation.org, 2018.

[29] Technological development is creating a habit whereby relationships are formed more and more via technology and less and less via physical human interaction. The psychologist Sherry Turkle studied the phenomenon and exposed it in the book *Alone Together: Why We Expect More from Technology and Less from Each Other*, New York, Basic Books, 2011.

[30] "I hope I live long enough not to die."

[31] Updated statistics: World Health Organization, "Road Traffic Injuries", who.int, 7 December 2018.

[32] US Department of Transportation, "Critical reasons for crashes investigated in the national motor vehicle crash causation survey", crashstats.nhtsa.dot.gov, 2015.

[33] Istat, "Incidenti stradali in Italia", 2018, available at www.istat.it.

[34] R. Lanctot et al., "Accelerating the future: The economic impact of the emerging passenger economy", strategyanalytics.com, 1 June 2017.

[35] A study released in *Nature* showed that the choice of who was more or less worthy of being saved varied greatly depending on the cultural background of the respondents. E. Awad, S. Dsouza et al., "The Moral Machine experiment", *Nature*, 563, 24 October 2018, 59-64.

[36] J. F. Bonnefon, A. Shariff and I. Rahwan, "The social dilemma of autonomous vehicles", *Science*, 352 (6293), 24 June 2016, 1573-1576. The study showed that potential travellers, while willing that others ride in vehicles that, in the event of a crash, sacrifice them to save others, would themselves prefer to ride in cars that protect their passengers at all costs.

[37] Schematic reproduction of the logic behind the artist's work: J. Bridle, "Autonomous Trap 001", 2017, video available at https://vimeo.com.

[38] Uber, for example, is already working on Uber Elevate, a passenger air transport service that works using the same logic as the famous service provided today with cars and yachts (currently with drivers).

[39] Moscow Institute of Physics and Technology (MFTI), May 2014.

3 Preparing for the Trip

Passports and documents

One of the comforts of travelling in the future is not having to worry about passports, identity cards and other documents. If this is your first time in 2050, on arrival you will be scanned and your details recorded in a few minutes: from then on, your medical and personal information will be uploaded to the network and shared by international control bodies. In this way, if you decide to visit other countries or in case of general checks, biometric detection devices will automatically be able to check your identity and verify that you are in good health and are complying with the rules. Even if stopped by the police or other authorities, you don't need to show any documents: the portable scanners use physical facial recognition, recovering all necessary data in an instant.

Emergencies

The year 2050 is a relatively safe place, crime and violence are rare and hardly ever involve tourists. Surveillance systems, police-robots, cameras and predictive algorithms can anticipate well in advance where and how crimes will occur. Cities exploit networks of video-microphone sensors capable of identifying in a fraction of a second gun noise, verbal arguments, fights and suspicious sounds. An artificial intelligence system analyses sounds and determines their point of origin, sending reports to the police, who are thus able to be at the scene of a crime very quickly.

When questioning suspects, the police will use devices and sensors to monitor their heart rate, breathing and blood pressure and expose any lies.

While traditional crimes are becoming increasingly rare, online crimes are occurring much more frequently. Thefts of DNA and identity are commonplace, as are online scams. Be warned, therefore, when surfing online or in virtual reality and avoid infamous or overcrowded places. If necessary, go to the computer police: hacker patrols dedicated to cybersecurity protection will be at your complete disposal.

(Lost and) found

One thing that is unlikely to happen to you on your journey in 2050 is that you lose something. Most of the objects we lose in the present no longer exist in 2050 and are no longer needed (wallets, keys and documents). Many tools and applications also make it easy to locate most things, such as means of transport, animals or people.

Communication

Shortening distances

In 2050 it is considered normal to be in two different places at the same time. The concept, however, should not be taken too literally: some technologies do allow you to be in multiple places at the same time, but not within your own body. Among these, the most widespread are telepresence, which uses static screens attached to the walls (or the screen of personal devices), and mobile tools: robots equipped with monitors, sensors and cameras, which become real physical avatars, able to interact with people, other robots and the environment. These inventions have revolutionized and redefined the concept of travel (work and pleasure), saving money, energy and time for companies, workers and people. Furthermore, by exploiting facial recognition software and other integrated tools, distance communication experiences are coming closer and closer to real meetings.

There is also the possibility of interacting in real time with objects and animals. Thanks to the Internet of Things, it's child's play to connect with cameras remotely and communicate with the washing machine, oven, fridge, TV, personal robot, dog or cat.

CONNECTED BRAINS

One of the most important areas of research in 2050 is so-called brain-to-brain communication. We have already talked about the brain–computer interface in Chapter 2, mentioning the technologies that allow one to read brainwaves. These tools are very useful for those who are unable to communicate because of serious illness. But what happens if this type of technology is developed in such a way as to be very precise, minimally invasive and affordable? Can we really imagine wearing special helmets that allow us to communicate without uttering a word? Well, in 2050 this option is considered very plausible thanks to historic pioneering studies that have paved the way for research.

Worthy of note is a scientific article, published in 2018, entitled "BrainNet: A Multi-Person Brain-to-Brain Interface for Direct Collaboration between Brains",[1] which showed how it was possible to record and provide information among the brains of three different subjects through magnetic resonance imaging and transcranial magnetic stimulation. Two of the three subjects were asked to play a game that was very similar to Tetris, and they made mental decisions about how to rotate the block displayed on a screen. The third subject, who did not see the screen, had to implement the decisions taken by the first two and received through stimulation. The results, although not 100 per cent accurate, showed that it was worthwhile to continue to explore this field.

One of the strongest moves in this direction has been by the European Human Brain Project, launched in 2013 with funds of about €1 billion, with the aim of achieving by 2023, through a supercomputer, a simulation of the full functioning of the human brain.

In 2050, everything you wear (watches, jewellery, clothes, necklaces) and everything around you has its own IP address and integrates with you,[2] helping you to send and receive communications, images, videos and messages.

Another way to communicate is through virtual meetings, which we have already talked about with regard to interpersonal relations. These meetings, facilitated by virtual reality, can be very realistic and are used for all types of interaction.

Compatibility of technological devices

The devices of 2050 are very different from those of 2020. For this reason, as soon as you arrive in the future, the suggestion is to go to an electronics store that will to supply you with adapters and useful tools, in particular sensors for food analysis (already mentioned in Chapter 2) and wearable and portable devices for communication, identity recognition, payments and networking. Without these objects, not only would your stay be limited and difficult, but you would also be a social outcast, as you would have a hard time interacting with the locals.

Hospitality

Even in 2050 there are hotels, campsites, apartments and shared rooms available for tourists or business visitors to rent.

The speed of transport and the ease of communication have reduced the need for long business trips, but some people still choose not to return home to sleep. In any case, try out at least a couple of the solutions available for overnight stays: many, for those who come from the past, will be unforgettable experiences.

Home as a service

One of the most numerous communities is that of the "nomads": homeless people who travel the planet using different subscription formulas per night. Housing, in this case, has turned into a service. For this reason, even those who decide to have a more stable life consider it normal to rent out their apartment when they are not at home. It is therefore very easy to find the right apartment for your needs using apps.

Smart home

The apartments in the richest cities are all smart homes and are fully automated. It is normal to live in buildings with roofs that change position to capture the sun's rays and regulate the internal temperature, filters that automatically purify the air, boxes that open by themselves, refrigerators that order food on the basis of biometric surveys of the bathroom (establishing the state of physical health of the inhabitants of the house), integrated security systems with facial recognition and artificial intelligence systems.

There are no "useless" objects: they all do something intelligent. Any examples? The alarm clock that sets itself, according to our habits and the commitments marked on the calendar, the automatic coffee maker, that prepares the coffee in synchronization with the alarm clock, the irrigation system that switches on only when needed, the lemon plant that warns us when it is time to prune it, or the mattress that turns by itself according to the change of season, based on the weather and temperature forecasts.

Co-living

Many inhabitants of 2050 live alone, in buildings structured to accommodate small private apartments and large common areas. These buildings become real communities over time, grouped according to lifestyle: there are some for young people, for the elderly and in some cases also for families with children. All facilities offer, according to requirement, spaces for leisure time, medical and health support, kindergartens, and cleaning and babysitting services.

Hotels and resorts

Hotels are fully automated and do not require service personnel. Like many public places, they have preferred to evolve towards a model that exploits the efficiencies of robots, using them for cleaning, payment, room service and catering.

In some countries, for the most nostalgic, there are still traditional hotels. Be careful, however, if you decide to stay in such a hotel, expect a heavy bill. As the use of human resources is considered a luxury and commands very high prices.

ONCE AGAIN ALICIA CALLED TO TESTIFY

Customers don't seem to have got it into their heads: Alicia, the artificial intelligence device who runs the house, is always listening and is the ideal witness in cases of domestic violence. Once again, therefore, Alicia has been called to the witness stand: during a trial in Australia she has allowed access to her recordings, helping to solve a case of attempted murder.

Notes

[1] L. Jiang, A. Stocco et al., "BrainNet: A Multi-Person Brain-to-Brain Interface for Direct Collaboration between Brains", *Scientific reports*, 9 (1), 2019, 6115.

[2] An IP address, Internet Protocol Address, is a numeric code that uniquely identifies a networked object.

4 The Future

*I'm interested in the future,
because that's where I'll spend
the rest of my life.*
Charles Franklin Kettering

*The best way to predict the future
is to create it.*
Abraham Lincoln

*The future is already here,
It's just not very evenly distributed.*
William Gibson

The future is always with us

The world in which we live is complex and every moment our brain receives a rush of stimuli, information, images and sounds. If we had to pay attention to everything, we would not be able to act or think. One of the most precious activities carried out by our brain is precisely the "sorting": without us realizing, it makes a selection of the information and brings to our attention only the most important, that is, those that will impact more significantly on the present or on the future. When we wear a T-shirt, after a few seconds we stop noticing the cotton that touches our skin, because it is not important to think about it all the time; when we are watching a movie we do not perceive all the small noises that come from the street and from our house; when we hear a news item on the TV, we unconsciously assess its impact on our lives and weigh it up accordingly. This process takes place continuously and is the result of the interaction between the brain and the five senses. And so, at all times, we take small and big decisions, based on complex assessments made by our brain considering the risks, opportunities, benefits and damages that may result from our actions or those of others.

Let's take an example (Figure 23). It's Sunday, and we decided to visit a farm in the country. What is the likelihood that we will encounter a lion, a dog or a lamb respectively? And, if we meet them, the likelihood it will create a dangerous situation? On the basis of the answers to these two questions, we will assess the level of priority and decide how concerned we are about a possible meeting. Let us therefore proceed in order. It is not often that a lion is seen on a farm, so even if it is a very dangerous beast, there is no point in worrying about it. The lamb, on the contrary, is a docile animal and does not represent a threat, even if it is very likely that we shall meet it. Almost certainly, there will be a dog, which, being domesticated and in many cases in a lead, should not be a problem. We know, however, that the dog does not know us and for this reason it may feel threatened by our presence and decide to attack us. Although the risk is moderate, therefore, it is better to be alert, and consider running into a potentially dangerous dog as a possible scenario.

Figure 23 Concern and probability

	Lion	Dog	Lamb
Hazard level 0 to 10	10	4	2
Probability of meeting	0	8	1
EXPECTED DAMAGE	0	32	2

Now let's try to think of a more distant future. Think climate change, the risks of genetic experimentation, the challenges posed by demographic growth and the exploitation of resources. Let's think about the possibility that a meteor will hit our planet, that the Earth's magnetic field will be reversed or that the Yellowstone super volcano will explode. Think of the possibility of developing super bacteria resistant to any antibiotic and the associated risk of a pandemic. These are episodes which would have enormous impacts on the whole of humanity, but which we tend not to include in our list of daily priorities. Why is that? Because these are events that we perceive are far away, and we cannot grasp the effects that they could have on our lives. Moreover, our perception leads us to believe that we cannot influence major changes and that it is therefore not worth committing our time and efforts in an attempt to understand them and change their course. And yet, if we think about it rationally, we are dealing with eventualities and problems that we must address as soon as possible.

The truth is that we are less rational beings than we believe and often act on the basis of instincts, sensations and perceptions, which have nothing to do with probabilistic calculations and objective decision-making processes. After all, many of the processes involved in this mechanism are still not clear to us: what weight do reason and instinct carry in our decision-making? Let's try to reflect on how many times a decision taken on impulse, without thinking too much about it, has turned out to be the right one. In all these cases, we have been able to act in the best way even in the absence of structured and rational thought.

When it comes to the future, it is precisely our perceptions that play a fundamental role, because they have the power to decisively influence our ability to weigh priorities and to assign the right degree of attention to different issues.

No one can predict the future, it is true, but all of us can build models within which we can practise thinking about tomorrow. In this way we can define and evaluate new realities and new descriptive scenarios, able to tell us how we will live in the future, how our planet will be, what rules will guide our lives and what will be the future effect of the choices and decisions we make today.

These models are not only useful, therefore, but are also necessary, for consciously choosing the decisions that affect them will make our future even more difficult. Without it, we're like a ship navigating by sight, with no compass and no map.

Statistics tell us that governments, too often, end up planning on horizons of only four or five years and managers on horizons of nine months. In this way, it is difficult to make a statement, reason and take a motivated position on important issues such as whether or not robots have rights or responsibilities, the opportunity to use new technologies for health or the possibility of obliging all citizens of a country to submit to DNA testing. It is difficult to think about how we are going to solve the problem of climate change, what we are going to eat, how our homes are going to be: all issues that are essential for our future and that we have to deal with here and now.

Creating the future by telling stories

Have you ever noticed that we often make self-fulfilling prophecies? If we think that we will certainly lose a tennis match, we will be unlikely to find the strength to fight to the end; if we are convinced that something is impossible, we will give up every attempt to do it; if voters believe that a party will not gain enough votes and that therefore it is not worth voting for, they will choose another side and consequently their original party of choice will not win. We could give dozens of examples of this kind. It is not a question of objective and correct forecasts at the outset, but of situations influenced by our judgement, more than we realize.

The future, then, is also the result of our predictions and one way to start to influence it positively is to try to imagine it as we would like it to be. This is the first step in making it happen. No one realizes a future that they dare not even imagine.

Too much talk about broad-minded and generic futures (climate change will increasingly melt the ice of the Arctic Ocean, artificial intelligence will change the way we work in the next hundred years) does not help us to contextualize and really understand what we are talking about. With a bit of storytelling, instead, we can think about the future, perceive the changes that need to be made to achieve this (even in the smallest details) and give free rein to the imagination.

This exercise has three main ingredients:

- *Group work*: individual choices also influence the lives of others and their point of view is valuable to achieve the most complete picture possible. The future is open source.
- *Creativity*: creatives are those who sees a different future to others and decide to realize it. Like Steve Jobs, who saw a future with a

phone without a keyboard, or like Elon Musk, who believes in a future in which electric cars are able to compete in the market with luxury cars.
- *Critical spirit*: when we talk about the future, the world is divided between optimists and pessimists, between those who believe that, thanks to science and technology, we will be able to solve the great challenges of humanity, and those who think that nothing will change, that problems will increase and that our well-being decrease. Utopias versus dystopias. So science fiction films propose worlds in which everything has gone wrong, while the protagonists of technological progress actually spread their visions of the future, to the cry of "Let's make the world a better place."[1] And we divide ourselves between the two sides, following little more than our perceptions, when instead we have, with a little knowledge and critical spirit, all the tools to understand that the future will be neither the one nor the other.

Technology and inventions

When we think about the future, technology and inventions occupy most of our thoughts. This is because scientific and technological inventions often interrupt continuity, changing our way of being and living on the planet. Thus, we often end up associating them almost exclusively with the future, as if they were the only important element to consider. But if we want technology to be a tool, then we need to be able to talk about society and the impacts we expect on our lives: this is what really counts.

Just because something is technically possible doesn't mean it has to be done. It is we who decide how to use a given invention, we are responsible for assessing, with caution and attention, the desired and unwanted impacts that can bring with it.

Today, technological instruments support us in many situations and, in some way, "govern" us as laws do, because not only has our physical world changed, but also our ethical, moral and legal world. Technological tools profoundly change who we are, our brains, our habits, our way of living and interacting with each other and with the outside world. I have seen this by dealing with the mutations in the brains of new generations, the implications related to reproductive changes and relational behaviour, and psychological diseases derived from the use of virtual and augmented reality. These are central themes in the history of mankind, which have and will have enormous impacts on our lives. But, because of the generational change, we still tend not to worry enough about it.

Responsibility

The period in which we live has been characterized by a great penetration of technology into people's lives. These technologies are a way of enhancing our physical and cognitive abilities and can, in some cases, assign great power to individuals, for better or for worse. Small groups of hackers can sabotage the activities of entire airlines, just as a minor can block a global cyber-attack on his or her own.

It is therefore particularly important to establish and define an ethics of responsibility, capable of taking into account those actions and consequences that can be strengthened today as never before in the history of mankind.

In 1919, Max Weber theorized an ethics of responsibility, linking it to the ethics of the political man who follow his own choices because he is able, thanks to his position of power, to influence the destiny of the world. Today, this concept must apply to all citizens, because, thanks to technology, we all potentially have the same ability to change the world.

Scientists, researchers and technology experts have the responsibility to live an active political and social life, to help the wider community understand possible future scenarios through debate, dissemination and training.

Responsibility is not only for the present, but also for future generations, in the interests of which we have a very serious and social obligation to work together, to imagine and build the best of possible futures.

Note

[1] "Let's make the world a better place": this is one of the most pertinent mottos from the technology start-ups of Silicon Valley and around the world.

Glossary of the Future

Algorithm
A systematic method used in the field of computer science to solve a problem or calculate a result by applying a certain number of orders, instructions and conditions set in advance.

Anthropocene
Term coined in 1980s by the biologist Eugene Stoermer, indicates the current geological era, in which humans and their activities are considered the main causes of territorial, structural and climatic changes.

Artificial intelligence
The ability of a computer to perform typical functions and reasoning completely autonomously, without any need for a human controller. Machines equipped with artificial intelligence in 2050 are capable of making decisions, automatically solving problems and learning. This often makes it difficult to distinguish a robot from a living being.

Augmented reality
Technology that allows normal reality to be enriched with artificial and virtual information, superimposing data, images and projections. The most famous example nowadays is Google Glass: special glasses that, through semi-transparent displays, allow the real–virtual combination.

Big data
Technologies and methodologies for the aggregation and analysis of massive data.

Biohacker and biohacking

Biohackers are people and communities that undertake biological research in a way similar to that of a computer hacker, that is, outside laboratories or institutions and in an open and horizontal form. It is a practice that raises many ethical doubts and concerns about the possible consequences of experiments that have gone wrong and have been carried out without proper scientific supervision.

Blockchain

A database, distributed among many computers around the world, which records and archives transactions that take place within the network, eliminating the need for third-party intermediaries (such as banks). The particularity of the blockchain, conceived and released on the net through an anonymous scientific article published under the pseudonym of Satoshi Nakamoto in 2009, is to be a safe and impregnable protocol, which eliminates the risks of fraud and scams. Because of these characteristics, it is used in the financial sector, in transactions and transfers of ownership and for the storage of certificates and personal data.

Bot

Bots (abbreviation of robot) are software that, using artificial intelligence and machine learning, can perform various tasks completely independently.

There are different types of bots, depending on their ability. The most popular are undoubtedly the chatbots: conversational algorithms used to interact with human beings and respond to their needs through messaging platforms.

Brain–computer interface

See *Neurotechnologies*.

Chatbot

See *Bot*.

Chimera

A chimera is a living being resulting from the union of genetic or biological materials of different species.

Cloud computing
Remotely using software and hardware resources (e.g., data storage) by paying for the service, usually by subscription.

CRISPR-CAS9
Clustered Regularly Interspaced Short Palindromic Repeats is a very precise genetic editing technique that is able, in an economical and easy way, to eliminate defective genes and repair a problematic genome by modifying it permanently.

Crowdfunding
Also known as "collective financing", this is a fundraising process, mostly via the Internet, that takes place through the small financial contributions of individuals or groups of people who share a common interest or who wish to support an innovative idea of a third party.

Cryptocurrencies
These are virtual coins, protected and secured using the principles of cryptography. Like any digital currency, cryptocurrency allows people to make secure and anonymous online payments. Cryptocurrencies can be used to buy real products or can be exchanged for real money (euros, dollars, pounds sterling etc.).

Cyborg
Living organism, human or animal, to which limbs, artificial prostheses or synthetic organs have been transplanted.

Drone
Flying object controlled remotely or equipped with artificial intelligence. It is used for military, film or transport purposes. In 2050, almost all deliveries are made by drone.

Encryption
Encryption is a technique that allows you to send a private message through the use of a secret code. Only those who are in possession of the code to decipher the message will be able to read it.

Enhancement

This is defined as temporary or definitive attempts to modify the human body by overcoming natural limits (physical or cognitive) through natural or artificial means. Often contrasted with treatment, the boundary between the two is very fluid and lies in the subject and in the objectives of the application: the same medicine or technology generates enhancement if used on a healthy subject, while it is considered a cure if used on somene who is ill or suffering.

Functional food

Foods considered by scientists to positively influence the state of health and well-being of the human body. Functional foods of 2050 have often undergone genetic modification to improve their ability to reduce or prevent the onset of disease in humans.

Fyborg

The term coined by Alexander Chislenko identifies human beings who exploit and use technologies such as contact lenses, smartphones and hearing aids to improve their capabilities or correct physical imperfections.

Genetics

Genetics (from the ancient Greek *ghenetikós*, "relative to birth", from *ghénesis*, "genesis, origin") is a branch of biology that studies the mechanisms underlying genes and gene inheritance and variability in living organisms, trying to understand the rules concerning the transmission of biological characteristics from one generation to the next in the various animal and plant species. Following the discovery, in 1940s, that the physical basis of the inheritance is preserved within DNA, *molecular genetics* was born: a discipline that, through the manipulation of the information contained in DNA, aims to correct physical malformations and predisposition to disease.

Genomics

Genomics is a branch of molecular biology that studies the genome of living organisms, analysing the latter's structure, content, function and evolution. Among the objectives of genomics, the most important is the creation of genetic and physical maps of the DNA of living organisms.

Internet of Things
The possibility to network and connect objects and devices, wherever they are, making them "intelligent": able to "think" by themselves, interact with other objects and collect data and information.

Mutant
A human being or an animal carrying one or more gene mutations which, by giving it new characteristics, make it more or less suitable for survival. Within a population mutants appear randomly and spontaneously, but in 2050 the mutation can also occur on request, by manipulating the DNA.

Nanotechnologies
A branch of applied science that deals with the control of matter on a dimensional scale of less than one billionth of a metre, and with its design and implementation, including the use of advanced technologies, instruments and devices on that scale.
  Technological development has made it possible to use nanotechnologies to create equipment and instruments capable of seeing, investigating, manipulating and controlling matter on an atomic scale, with the possibility of unprecedented applications in materials technologies, electronic computers, medicine and biology, environment and energy, chemistry, mechanics, aeronautics and the automotive sector.

Neural interface
See *Neurotechnologies*.

Neurotechnologies
These are technical and computer tools that interact with the nervous system of living beings, managing to correct any malfunctions or expand capabilities. Among the most common neurological features are *neuroprostheses*, which use electronic devices to correct the functions of the nervous system or damaged sensory organs, and *brain–computer interfaces*, which allow the brain to communicate directly with an external computer device. There are many areas of application, such as the correction of vision and hearing dysfunctions, the possibility of modifying the perception of pain and the sense of hunger, increasing the ability to move and to remember, and effectively managing anxiety.

Quantum computer

This is a computer that exploits the laws of physics and quantum mechanics for data processing. It is based on a basic unit called *qubit* (in normal computers the unit is the bit). The qubits exceed the binary logic of the bits and can assume several states at the same time (the bit can assume only state 0 or state 1, alternatively). Result? A much more powerful and faster computer, capable of supporting complex software and overcoming the physical limitations of computers on the market today.

Quantum internet

One of the fascinating things about quantum physics is that if the parts of the cells are connected together, it doesn't matter how far apart they are – what happens to one happens to the other. This phenomenon is called *entanglement*. We can imagine the photons entangled (subject to the property of *quantum entanglement*) as envelopes that carry our messages, protecting them with a special encryption. Since in quantum physics you are not able to ascertain the status of information until you look at it, and the act of looking at it has the effect of changing it, the interesting thing is that when a sender uses a cryptographic key encoded in a quantum signal for a message, if anybody tries to intercept the key, they will destroy the message.

By combining these two features – the security of confidential information and the fact that it is not necessary for the information to cover kilometres – it is possible to obtain a more secure way of sending information. At the time of writing, the quantum internet is in an embryonic phase of experimentation in Chicago, China and Washington.

Smart cities

Smart cities are intelligent cities, built and developed according to urban design strategies based on efficiency, management, active citizen participation and the use of the most modern information and communication technologies. In smart cities, for example, waste collection is self-propelled and uses intelligent transport, and digital communications on smartphones and tablets allow total control of traffic and the sharing of tourist, cultural or commercial information via the Internet. The ultimate aim of these cities is to improve the quality of human life in a sustainable urban context.

Stem cells

There are two types of stem cells: embryonic, which derive from a blastocyst, an early-stage pre-implantation embryo, and adult. Stem cells are very valuable, because they function as a wild card: they can transform into any other cell, from a muscle cell to a gastric wall cell. In 2050 some of the fields of application of stem cells are:

- assisted reproduction;
- use in the brain to combat aging;
- production of organs and other biological elements printed in 3D;
- creation of animal proteins in the laboratory for food and medical purposes.

Terraforming

This is a means by which to change the climate, topography or ecology of a planet so that it is better suited to sustaining life.

Transhumanists

Transhumanists are in favour of the invasive use of technology to try to improve their physical and cognitive conditions and extend their life span: one way is through the transfer of human consciousness into mechanical hardware.

Virtual reality

Realistic simulation of a reality that does not exist, virtual reality consists of a three-dimensional computer-built environment that can be explored and with which it is possible to interact using computer devices (such as eyewear, gloves, earphones) that project the wearer into a scenario so realistic as to seem true. In virtual reality, in addition to images, sounds, tastes, scents, smells and tactile sensations can be reproduced.

Bibliography

Preliminary Remarks

P. Bishop, "Framework forecasting. Managing uncertainty and influencing the future", paper presented at Second Prague Workshop on Futures Studies Methodology, October 2005.
P. Borel, *Discours nouveau prouvant la pluralité des mondes* (1657), ed. A. Del Prete, Lecce, Conte, 1998.
T. Campanella, *La città del sole* [The City of the Sun] (1602), edited by N. Bobbio, Turin, Einaudi, 1941.
J. Hughes, *Citizen Cyborg: Why Democratic Societies Must Respond to the Redesigned Human of the Future*, Cambridge (MA), Westview Press, 2004.
IBM Marketing Cloud, "10 Key Marketing Trends for 2017 and Ideas for Exceeding Customer Expectations", comsenseconsulting.com, 2017.
R. Kurzweil, *The Singularity is Near: When Humans Transcend Biology*, New York, Viking, 2005.
V. Vinge, "The coming technological singularity: How to survive in the post-human era", conference paper, Department of Mathematical Sciences San Diego State University, 1993.
D. Wolens, "Singularity 101 with Vernor Vinge", *H+ Magazine*, 22 April 2009.

Chapter 1

AFP, "Fly me to the Moon: For some, lunar village takes shape", phys.org, 22 September 2017.
A. Bazzi, "Pacemaker messi fuori uso dagli hacker: rischio reale per i pazienti?" [Pacemakers hacked: a real risk for patients?], *Corriere della Sera*, 21 February 2018.
Black Mirror, Season 3, Episode 1, "Nosedive", 21 October 2016, available at netflix.com.
L. Clark, "Cyborgs like us", 2018, abstract available at thewire.ch.

P. Crutzen, *Benvenuti nell'Antropocene. L'uomo ha cambiato il clima, la Terra entra in una nuova era* [Welcome to Anthropocene! Man has changed the climate: earth enters a new era], Milan, Mondadori, 2005.

R. Dawkins, "A.I. might run the world better than humans do", video available at bigthink.com, 23 September 2017.

T. De Chant, "The world population, concentrated", persquaremile.wordpress.com, 18 January 2011.

D. Eggers, *The Circle*, New York, Alfred A. Kopf, 2013.

M. Gabanelli, A. Marinelli, "Genetica in garage: i rischi di modificare il dna in casa" [Genetics in the garage: The risks of modifying DNA at home], *Corriere della Sera*, 2 October 2018.

J. Gallagher, "Same-sex mice have babies", bbc.com, 11 October 2018.

C.S. Green, D. Bavelier, "Action video game modifies visual selective attention", *Nature*, 423 (6369), 29 May 2003, 534-537.

M. Grooten, R.E.A. Almond (eds.), *Living Planet Report 2018: Aiming Higher*, Gland, WWF, 2018.

Y.N. Harari, *Homo Deus. A Brief History of Tomorrow*, London, Harvill Secker, 2016.

D. Hoornweg, K. Pope, "Socioeconomic Pathways and Regional Distribution of the World's 101 Largest Cities", Global Cities Institute Working Paper No. 4, 2014 (abstract available at shared.uoit.ca).

Istat, "Popolazione residente per stato civile" (Resident population by marital status), September 2018, available at istat.it.

I. Johnston, "Life on Mars: City of a million people could be built on Red Planet by 2062, says Elon Musk", *The Independent*, 22 June 2017.

A.J. Latham, L.L.M. Patston, L.J. Tippett, "The virtual brain: 30 years of video-game play and cognitive abilities", *Frontiers of Psychology*, 4, September 2013, 629.

D. Levy, *Love and Sex with Robots: The Evolution of Human-Robot Relationships*, New York, HarperCollins, 2009.

C. Newton, "Speak, Memory. When her best friend died, she rebuilt him using artificial intelligence", theverge.com, October 2016.

S. Petrucciani, *Marx*, Rome, Carocci, 2009.

Pew Research Center, "The future of world religions: Population growth projections, 2010-2050", pewforum.org, 2 April 2015.

Statista, "The most spoken languages worldwide (native speakers in millions)", statista.com, 2018.

L. Streondj, "A home for robots or-else artilect war!", joylifecoop.wordpress.com, 3 January 2016.

TEDGlobal, "Pia Mancini: How to upgrade democracy for the Internet era", 2014, video available at ted.com.

United Nations, "Concluding session to draft marine biodiversity treaty, conference president says environmental impact assessments will be reflected in instrument", un.org, 17 September 2018.

United Nations, Department of Economic and Social Affairs, "World Urbanization Prospects", 2018 Revision, data set, population.un.org, 2018.

United Nations, Department of Economic and Social Affairs, Population Division, "World Population Prospects: Key Findings and Advance Tables", 2017 Revision, Working Paper No. ESA/P/WP/248, 2017 (available at esa.un.org).

G. Vince, "The Biosphere", in J. Al-Khalili (ed.), *What's Next*, London, Profile Books, 2017.

J.E.M. Watson, J.R. Allan *et al.*, "Protect the last of the wild", *Nature*, 563 (7729), November 2018, 27-30.

WR, The Institute of digital democracy, "Cost of voting. Estimating the impact of online voting on public finance," 2017.

F. Xiang, "AI will spell the end of capitalism", *Washington Post*, 3 May 2018.

Chapter 2

E. Awad *et al.*, "The Moral Machine experiment", *Nature*, 563, 24 October 2018, 59-64.

J.-F. Bonnefon, A. Shariff, I. Rahwan, "The social dilemma of autonomous vehicles", *Science*, 352 (6293), 24 June 2016, 1573-1576.

J. Bridle, "Autonomous Trap 001", 2017, video available at vimeo.com.

F. Franzosi *et al.*, "An innovative approach to the assessment of hydro-political risk: A spatially explicit, data driven indicator of hydro-political issues", *Science Direct, Global Environmental Change*, 52, 2018, 286-313.

B. Gallagher, "So can we terraform Mars or not?", *Nautilus*, 11 October 2018.

Institution of Mechanical Engineers, "Global food: Waste not, want not", imeche.org, 2 November 2013.

Istat, "Incidenti stradali in Italia" [Road accidents in Italy], 2018, available at istat.it.

L. Jiang, A. Stocco *et al.*, "BrainNet: A multi-person brain-to-brain interface for direct collaboration between brains", *Scientific reports*, 9 (1), 2019, 6115.

K. Korosec, "Russia is planning to build a luxury hotel on the International Space Station", *Fortune*, 28 December 2017.

E. Kovačič (ed.), "Scienziati dell'Istituto di Fisica e Tecnologia di Mosca avverano il Teletrasporto" [Scientists of the Institute of Physics and Technology of Moscow make Teleportation come true], segnidalcielo.it, 18 July 2014.

R. Lanctot *et al.*, "Accelerating the future: The economic impact of the emerging passenger economy", strategyanalytics.com, 1 June 2017.

C. Lippert , R. Sabatini *et al.*, "Identification of individuals by trait prediction using whole-genome sequencing data", PNAS, 114 (38), September 2017, 19.

C. Parmesan, G. Yohe, "A globally coherent fingerprint of climate change impacts across natural systems", *Nature*, 421 (6918), January 2003, 37-42.

E. Peper, R. Harvey, "Digital addiction: increased loneliness, anxiety, and depression", neuroregulation.org, 2018.
T.L. Root et al., "Fingerprints of global warming on wild animals and plants", *Nature*, 421 (6918), January 2003, 57-60.
S. Roversi, "Future food for climate change: le grandi sfide del food tech", *Nòva*, 7 June 2018.
L.C. Smith, *The World in 2050: Four Forces Shaping Civilization's Northern Future*, New York, Dutton Books, 2010.
Systems Analysis and Concepts Directorate, "High Altitude Venus Operational Concept (HAVOC)", sacd.larc.nasa.gov, 13 December 2018.
S. Turkle, *Alone Together: Why We Expect More from Technology and Less from Each Other*, New York, Basic Books, 2011.
US Department of Transportation, "Critical reasons for crashes investigated in the National Motor Vehicle Crash Causation Survey", crashstats.nhtsa.dot.gov, 2015.
A. Van Huis, J. Van Itterbeeck et al., *Edible Insects: Future Prospects for Food and Feed Security*, Rome, FAO, 2013.
World Health Organization, "Road traffic injuries", who.int, 7 December 2018.

Other recommended readings

D. Adams, *The Hitchhiker's Guide to the Galaxy*, New York, Harmony Books, 1980.
N. Agar, *The Skeptical Optimist: Why Technology Isn't the Answer to Everything*, Oxford, Oxford University Press, 2015.
J. Al-Khalili, *What's Next? Even Scientists Can't Predict the Future – Or Can They?*, UK, Profile Books Ltd, 2017.
J. Barrat, *Our Final Invention*, New York, Thomas Dunne Books, 2013.
N. Bostrom, *Superintelligence: Paths, Dangers, Strategies*, Oxford, Oxford University Press, 2014.
N. Chomsky, *What Kind of Creatures Are We?*, New York, Columbia University Press, 2016.
P.S. Churchland, *Braintrust: What Neuroscience Tells Us about Morality*, Princeton, Princeton University Press, 2011.
A. Da Re, *Filosofia morale* [Moral philosophy], Milan, Mondadori, 2003.
L. De Biase, *Homo Pluralis. Esseri umani nell'era tecnologica* [Homo Pluralis. Human beings in the technological age], Turin, Codice, 2015.
P. Diamandis, *Abundance. The Future Is Better than You Think*, New York, Free Press, 2012.
P. Diamandis, S. Kotler, *Bold: How to Go Big, Achieve Success, and Impact the World*, New York, Simon & Schuster, 2015.
M. Ford, *Rise of the Robots, Technology and the Threat of a Jobless Future*, New York, Basic Books, 2015.

M. Goodman, *Future Crimes*, New York, Anchor Books-Penguin Random House, 2015.

H.T. Greely, *The End of Sex and the Future of Human Reproduction*, Cambridge & London, Harvard University Press, 2016.

J.N. Harari, *Sapiens: A Brief History of Humankind* (2011), London, Vintage, 2015.

S. Jasanoff, *The Ethics of Invention: Technology and the Human Future*, New York-London, W.W. Norton & Company, 2016.

R. Kurzweil, *How to Create a Mind: The Secret of Human Thought Revealed*, New York, Viking Press, 2012.

R. Kurzweil, *The Age of Spiritual Machines*, London, Phoenix, 1999.

New Scientist, *The Universe Next Door*, Great Britain, Hodder & Stoughton, 2017.

R. Oldani, *Spaghetti robot. Il made in Italy che ci cambierà la vita* [Spaghetti robot. The made in Italy that will change our lives], Turin, Codice, 2014.

G. Orwell, *Nineteen Eighty-Four*, London, Secker and Warburg, 1949.

H. Rheingold, *Net Smart*, Cambridge, The Mitt Press, 2012 .

A. Ross, *The Industries of the Future*, London, Simon & Schuster, 2016.

D. Van Reybrouck, *Against Elections: The Case for Democracy*, London, The Bodley Head, 2013.

D. Wolman, *The End of Money*, Boston, Da Capo Press, 2012.

I. Yeoman, *2050 Tomorrow's Tourism*, Bristol, Channel View Publications, 2012.

www.ingramcontent.com/pod-product-compliance
Lightning Source LLC
LaVergne TN
LVHW090606160426
836500LV00028B/217